Hard Edge

Part 1: Forging the Steel

Conrad Lockston

COLOURBLUE PRESS

https://www.colour-blue.co.uk

© Conrad Lockston/Chris McNab, 2022

ISBN: 9798353995166

Readers interested in other titles from Colourblue Press should visit our website at https://www.colour-blue.co.uk

Cover photo by Stewart Hanman

Cover design by Nigel Sykes

Contents

INTRODUCTION

It was the summer in the 1990s, and every day brought a new fucking adventure. It seemed like I was a magnet for fists, boots and blood. Let me give you an example. There was this one day on the seafront in *A*—, and some lads, real pieces of shit, had pushed a guy off the seawall. Bear in mind this is a 20ft drop onto rocks. So, I decided to do the whole white knight thing, and I went to help the fella out.

It all came to a head outside a fucking kebab shop, the classic street amphitheatre, where the lads had gone inside. As I approached, they puffed their chests out and came out mouthing off at me. It was the usual stuff, telling me to go fuck myself. Get this – one of them obviously thought he was full ninja and said, 'I do karate.' as if I would shit myself and run off. He doesn't know that I've already got two black belts in that stuff and a back catalogue of more than a decade of street fighting. Anyway, the silly cunt locks and loads and decides to have a go.

Turns out, he was a prime fucking example of how doing a martial art badly can screw up your street fighting. As he went to hit me, he pulled his fist back to his hip, completely telegraphing what he was intending to do. He may as well have sent up a naval flare to warn me in advance. I think I had time to go put the kettle on and ponder my next move. As he cocked his arm, I simply leaned forward and grabbed him by the crook of

1

his elbow. He instantly looked like a right twat – now he simply couldn't follow through with the punch, plus one of his arms was out of action. But he didn't have much time to reflect.

At almost the same instant as I grabbed his elbow, I put my body into full torque and drove an absolute monster right elbow straight into his face. I swear the tip of my elbow broke the sound barrier, plus it was carrying all my sixteen stone in weight. Well, it was like he'd been poleaxed on a medieval battlefield. I smashed him so hard that not only did I obliterate his nose, but his legs came off the floor like a fucking jumpy puppet. His feet kept going into the air and whacked me with such force under my right shoulder that they left a massive bruise there, which stayed for about three weeks.

But as you'll see, people can take all sorts of shit and still get up. As he went down, he smashed his head on the floor at a nasty angle, but then for good measure I booted him in the face while his head was actually pressed up against the wall behind him. I have to say, the kick was fucking melon-crushing hard.

As this was happening, one of the guy's mates then decided he was the cavalry and came flying out the kebab shop at full cock. I switched targets quickly – as he opened the door I swung around and belted him in the face with a right cross. He went flying backwards, whacking his head on the door frame and breaking a window with one of his flailing arms. He was out. Job done.

The first guy on the floor became a concern. I thought he was dead, in fairness, I thought I'd killed him. A few minutes later, from a distance I saw the paramedics who were called putting him into an ambulance, his body covered with tubes and shit. I think they were also doing resuscitation on him. We fucked off pretty quick.

Okay, this was now getting serious. It got worse… I had a call saying he was dead. Christ, the awkward bastard! The next day, James and I went out training with the regional karate team, and while we were there, he was constantly on the phone, trying to find out whether this guy had really croaked or not. I was staring at the back-end of twenty-five years inside, and I was still in my late teens. Then I had a call telling me that his family had gone apeshit, and were driving around town beating up my mates, trying to flush me out for vengeance.

The word 'relief' simply doesn't capture the arse-loosening gratitude when I found out he wasn't dead after all. But now, I had a massive target on my back for all this fucker's friends and family. It was the beginning of a long feud. Having seen what I'd done to one of their own, they would never send a single person, always a large, tooled-up and mouthy gang. Even the police came to see me and basically said that the family had put out a hit on me. They recommended that I should leave town for a while, but the obstinate bastard in me decided to stay put. Bring it on, that's the way I generally look at life. Having said this, a couple of proper chiselled-up hard men, whom nobody in town recognised, had turned up and were wandering around looking for me. I was a little concerned.

Then one day, two hard men of the family wandered into the sports shop where I was working. From the moment they came in, I knew they weren't in the market for a new fucking hoody. The lead guy was mouthing off straight away, so I just thought I'd hit him early on and get it over with. Customer service definitely went out the window – I grabbed a football boot off one of the racks and raked the studs across his face, splitting his eye open. They legged it. But then I look outside, and across the road there appears to be a fucking invading Mongol army, there are so many of them. They are all tooled up – bats, chains, a proper mechanic's armoury – waiting for me to come out. They were here to kill me, no doubt. I'm in proper shit.

This is when I thank God that I've got some mates. I phoned James, brought him quickly up to speed, and let him know that I needed him to come fast in his car and rescue me. What I really needed was for some beefy four-wheel drive SUV with bull-bars and horns on the bonnet to come screeching in. What I got was James's shit little Fiat, the type your nan would drive incompetently on a Sunday. A budget vibrator has more power. A few minutes later, though, I hear this camp little car horn beeping like there's a madman behind the wheel, coming down the street, getting closer. James literally swung open the passenger door while driving and didn't even stop as he passed the shop, slowing down just enough so that I could leap into the vehicle. 'Leap' isn't exactly right – half of my body was still hanging out the car as James pulled away, my shoes scraping on the road like some fucking clown act. But despite the clumsy getaway, it worked – the gang receding in the rear-view mirror were fucking livid. I was fit to fight another day, but now it was getting serious.

* * *

Having just read the passage above, I want you to answer two questions about me, working off the initial evidence: 1) Am I normal? 2) Is my life normal? For a long time, I thought I could answer yes to both questions. Then, as I started to put a few years on my life, people around me began to say, 'You should write a book about your life, but it's a long fucking way from normal.' So it was time for reflection. Maybe everything I thought was regular life was actually out-the-ballpark crazy, a head-fuck thunderstorm of fighting and violence, sudden deaths, police raids, criminal activity, dodgy business deals, martial-arts victories, celebrity gossip, sex with stunning women, sex with ugly women, drugs, gangland enforcement, nightclub security, and a metric ton of other weird shit. Putting all this down on paper might be the only way to discover whether it was normal or not.

In the pages that follow, in this book and the volumes to follow, you'll see my life unfold along crazily erratic paths, bouncing like a pinball in all manner of directions. Yet I have realised that the constant aching drum beat of my life is violence – seeing it, feeling it and, above all, giving it out. It seems that I've been fighting all my days. The fights have ranged from pathetic scuffles resulting in minor fabric damage to proper life-and-death battles, producing life-changing injuries. But whereas even some local roughnecks might have two or three scraps a year, I have had literally thousands of fights since my early years. Almost every day, certainly every week, I've had to either use violence or threaten it. Truth be told, fighting to me is almost like a form of meditation – to me it feels almost calming and honest, in a dishonest and complex world. Plus, if you want to understand the nature of violence and how to fight, I do feel I have something to tell you.

So here is the beginning of my story. In this first book, we'll take you through my scrapping youth through to my equally violent early adulthood. At first, it was my intention to pack my entire life story in a single volume. Then I realised there was just too much to squash in comfortably, plus I keep adding new adventures all the time. More volumes will follow, and hopefully you'll come along for the ride.

Given that much of this book is about twatting people and getting up to all sorts of dodgy shit, I've had to make a lot of changes to names, places, times and other stuff. Many of the people in this book are still alive (not all though), and I've no desire to rake up old shit. Sometimes a place will just be replaced by a letter, to limit the opportunities for you detectives out there. Beyond this, it's told as faithfully as I remember it.

Be warned – I'm not going to flower my life up and present myself as a hero on some sort of journey to enlightenment. I've made plenty of mistakes and done stuff I'm not proud of, and I'm probably going to keep doing them. Quick example. When I was working on nightclub doors, one night I threw a guy out of a club. It was banal stuff – actually I threw out lots of people, and he was just one of a crowd of faces. After my shift, I went out to get some food. I found myself in a kebab shop – yes, one of those again. And as I turned around with my food, there was this guy there again. This time he had a wine glass in his hand, which he was trying to ram into my neck. In the nick of time I managed to get my arms up so it deflected the blow upwards. The glass sliced across the top of my head, leaving me with a wound and a scar that I have to this day. With blood streaming down my face, I beat the living shit out of him and his mate. I ended up with the two attackers on the floor while I was battering them with a stool. Then this random guy comes running out of the crowd, straight towards me. He looks serious. The adrenaline is running and I've got a lump of glass sticking out of my head, then I see this guy sprinting at me, so I spin around and smash him in the face as hard as I could. He'd down and out. Turns out he was an off-duty paramedic coming to see if I was okay. Fuck.

So, there's some proof that you are going to hear it all – the good, bad and very fucking ugly.

Enough talk. Put the fucking gloves on, get your guard up, and prepare to fight...

CHAPTER 1 FAMILY MADNESS

A great poet once wrote, *They fuck you up, your mum and dad*. I'm not making that up – it was a guy called Philip Larkin. Well, I guess I'm with you on that one, Phil.

My story begins like everyone's does – with family. My family was a big 'un. I've got five half-brothers and a half-sister. The boys came from my mum's side, and although they were half-brothers we always regarded each other as full brothers, despite the ton of shit they would frequently tip into my life over the years to come. My mum was born in Grangetown, Cardiff, and lived there most of her life. Family fuck-ups were something of a tradition – her dad buggered off when she was young. I say 'buggered off,' but he only lived about five miles away. Despite that I think I only met him about five times in my entire life. He left a mark on my mum though. She was very hung up on him, and thought he was amazing, but she barely ever saw him. She also had an uneasy relationship with her mother and brother. Her brother was a proper Cardiff headcase, but they were close, whereas my nan hated my mum.

In terms of personality type, my mum was basically like a dodgy Chinese firework, prone to blowing up and taking your face off. She could start a row with herself. My nan was the same, so it was never going to be easy. I've got to be honest – my mum crossed the line from feisty to nuts. She was known for being batshit crazy, but God forbid you ever told her that – she was good with her fists and whatever else came to hand. My wife is almost the only woman I know who hasn't had a kicking from my mum. To put my mum into perspective, I used to get calls from her all the time to do her 'favours.' And we're not talking about nipping down the shop clutching a couple of notes to buy twenty fags and a copy of *Take a Break*. One of those favours was: 'Could you burn the neighbours out?' because she just didn't like them. She would literally have a go at anybody, fearless. If she was right she was right, and if she was wrong she was right, so if she couldn't beat you with her words she'd beat you with her fists. Then she'd drive a car into you, reverse it back over you, and park it on top of you with the hazard lights on to make sure you were down. She also used to embellish things like crazy – she'd find a fiver and tell you she'd found fifty quid.

They built 'em tough in those days. She was blonde, only 5ft 1in tall, although she was… let's say, 'wide' – she wasn't a small woman, if you know what I mean. Think small, turbocharged battle tank and you are getting the idea. Proper South Wales mum, basically. Her hardness came from life experience – toughness was always hereditary in our part of the world. She married her first husband at sixteen and had twins at twenty, but one of them died at birth. Doing her bit for global population growth, however, I think she had four kids before she reached the age of twenty-five.

For money, she used to do factory work and similar stuff, but then she opened a guest house once she had separated from her husband. She did quite well out of it. (Despite being rough as fuck, my family have shown something of a knack for business.) At first it was essentially a dodgy bedsit with a few rooms. Then she bought the house next door and knocked through. This eventually became a full-blown hotel – she did have a bit of drive behind her (and as you'll see, that's rubbed off on me).

Despite having a pyrotechnic personality, she'd do anything for us lot. I could stagger in at three in the morning, barely able to speak my own name, with eight of my equally fucked-up mates and she'd get out of bed and make us all a full meal, no problem. If any of my pals were in trouble with the police, it was her they would ring. She'd get them corroborating evidence or an alibi to prize them out of the station – she could run rings around the cops. She'd also let just about anybody into the hotel, which was swings and roundabouts. We had a couple of guys living with us who became like family, while other guests looked at you with wild eyes, like they just fucked a corpse.

If you were in my mum's good books, she'd treat you like minor royalty. But the minute you fell out with her – and you would – you were fucked. She was viciously unforgiving. The problem was that nobody knew where she drew the line. It was very weird. In her world, if you were well-off you were a fucking snob, but if you were poor you were a fucking loser, and she didn't really like anyone in between. She was equal opportunities when it came to hating people. She could also be hilarious, so you could never figure her out. But because I was the baby of the family, I used to get special treatment. She could have caught me mid-stroke fucking a nun and would never believe it was me. And if I did do anything, it was fine, because in her mind it obviously needed doing.

Let's turn to my dad... here we go. My dad was born in Essex. He was just a fucking wide boy. Imagine an Arthur Daley type, all jangling gold and dodgy deals. He was a Teddy boy, 6ft tall, built like a brick shithouse. Seriously, he was ridiculously strong, in fact, he looked strong but he was even stronger than he looked. His dad was a bit of a naughty boy, and so was my dad, so he came with a lot of underworld links. There were moments of attempted respectability, though. He did army National Service in the 1950s but spent most of his time in military prison because he was in trouble all the time. He used to fight a lot, fuck a lot, and if anything wasn't nailed down, he would nick it and sell it.

Dad was a proper fucking womaniser, to the point at which it was embarrassing. I used to go into school and my mates would tell me that their father had walked on my dad fucking their mum. Everyone else finds it funny, but it wasn't to me. He's in his eighties now and people still say nostalgically, 'Oh, he was a hell of a boy.' But he wasn't. He would simply go into a pub, get hammered, carry on drinking, grope people's wives, throw glasses and fill people in with his fists (or get the crap beaten out of himself). He was always like an eighteen-year-old pumped on crystal meth. It didn't help that he was an alcoholic who also ran the hotel bar.

And what a bar. It was one of those classic 1970s British drinking holes – a bar a mile long, all optics, glasses, beer pumps, bottles and peanut displays featuring teenagers with big tits. My dad built this bar himself, and he was proper proud of it. It was like an architectural version of himself – lots of gold and flashing lights, gaudy as shit, and surrounded by an acre of beer-sticky carpet. My dad fitted right in against this backdrop, with his unbuttoned shirt, gold jewellery, big collar and quiff.

He was really flash. If my dad had won a million quid, he'd probably spend it all straight away on a gold watch as big as a railway station clock, so he could walk round town jangling it. If he bought a car for five grand, he'd tell you it cost ten grand. When my nan died, my dad got left a shitload of money – possibly the best part of £750,000, which was an epic amount of money in those days. Well, it was like he covered himself in glue and rolled through a jewellers. He was literally walking around with ten or twenty grand of cash in his pocket – because he could – with lots of big gold chains and other baubles. He was always the richest man on the council estate. He had to be the centre of attention. If he had a drink he'd buy everyone else in the bar one as well, but only to show that he was the big fucking man. But if two weeks later he's got no money and someone else doesn't buy him a drink, that's it, that guy would be on his hit list forever. He just didn't play by anybody else's rules and his rules were all about him.

The bar was his domain. There were always a lot of people around, but I don't think many of them actually liked my dad. A lot of people were decent with him only because they would get a slap if they weren't. I think many people were also just around to keep an eye on my mum, because my dad was a properly bad guy. I personally think he's autistic or something like that. He's selfish to a point where you actually think he might just be taking the piss. He has zero morals – like none at all. Needless to say, he's had a big effect on the man I am today. I certainly don't drink like my dad. But, God forbid, his genes are there – when I do drink, I turn into an absolute cunt.

My mum basically ran the hotel and the kitchens, and my dad ran the bar, both of them helped by my brothers. Everything was done by family and there were no external staff. In terms of other work, my dad was also a scaffolder for a few years, then he went into steel erecting. He was actually pretty good at building stuff and DIY. When they had the hotel he was a scaffolder by day and ran the bar at night, when he wasn't pissed. He was at times 'unemployed', but even then, he'd be working on the side as a bricklayer. You know the sort – every rough estate has got a few of them.

I didn't have much to do with my dad really, apart from the times he was beating the life out of me. He was always pissed and he was a violent drunk, so I just stayed out of his way if possible. If there was a woman around with loose knickers and low morals and he could get a shag, he was alright. But if there were no women around to bleed off that testosterone, he'd be a little bastard. He was horrible to the family – to my brothers especially, he was an absolute beast. On the day he got married to my mum, apparently, he walked up to my brothers after the ceremony and said, 'Right, now you lot are fucked!' He had two kids from a previous marriage (although they weren't around much when I was young). In fact, he was living with my mum for three months before she found out he had been married and had kids. Proper nice guy.

When it came to women, my dad was a cunt, but he and my mum never separated – in those days, when you got married, you got married for life. Problem was, my mum used to worship the ground he walked on. He could never do any wrong, even when it was obvious what he was up to. She knew what he was doing on the side with rough birds, she told me so. But I've since found out she was probably doing the same sort of thing anyway, but she was just better at hiding it. I even found out at my mum's funeral that my dad might not even be my real dad. Just another weird, shitty day to file away in my fucked-up library of memory.

I popped into the world on 7 December 1976 in Cardiff Royal Infirmary. My formative years were spent living in the hotel – I was there until I was about eight or nine. It was a mental place to grow up in. Every spectrum of society, high and low, drifted through the rooms over

15

the years. We had pop stars come to stay – there were the guys from Dexy's Midnight Runners, for example, while they were No. 1 in the charts in the 1980s. Instead of going to one of the big, plush hotels, they went to my parent's hotel to keep a low profile. Of course, one of my brothers went and told everyone, so we had crowds of shrieking fans storming the place. But we even had politicians. Prime Minister, James Callaghan, came to stay once – he actually popped next door to retrieve my brother's football. Conversely, we also had a lot of lorry drivers stay with us, and I was still in touch with one of them until a couple of years ago when he died. They came week in, week out, and when we finally left the hotel some of them used to come and visit us once a week and stay in our house – we were that close. I met some great people, and equally I met a lot of fuckers.

But the overarching theme of my early memories is just chaos. I can also remember being quite lonely, because they weren't any other children about. You could say that my parents were neglectful, because I was just left my own devices. I was often left with an older brother, who was twelve years older than me, and I experienced a lot of shit that five- or six-year-olds should never experience. In many ways I don't think it did me any favours, and I always struggled with people of my own age. I just wasn't used to having other kids around, and when they were about, I just wanted to fight their little faces.

Looking back, what was normal to me as a little kid was asylum insane in the grand scheme of things. Every weekend, for example, we had these monster parties in the bar in the hotel. My parents used to sponsor a few local football teams, and second-oldest brother, Bobby, was on one the teams. He was a decent player, but he was also known for being fierce on the pitch and in the pub, so he had a lot of rough-arse friends. Many of them would flood our bar for the weekend parties. I was this little kid lacing his way through the pissed-up crowds, taking it all in. I knew so many people it was like half of Cardiff were my siblings. I couldn't do a thing wrong – I got whatever I wanted because they were all pissed. I'd walk through the middle of the din and everybody would be chucking me beers even, though I was six years old, or slipping me a couple of quid.

That jolly sort of stuff was fine, but there was the other, darker side. I remember the huge parties and big family gatherings at Christmas, everybody in the bar with their wives and kids. All cheering and hugs. Then a heartbeat later they were all trying to glass one another. The tension used to build, you could feel it, I still can to this day. The minute my dad had a drink he was an absolute pantomime monster – he was the match that lit the leaking gas.

Don't get me wrong, there were some stable presences in my life. I used to be close to my nan on my mum's side, for example. She didn't live far from us, and I can remember going around there as a kid. She used to have a boyfriend with a budgie, and I'd sit and play with the bird. She was no pushover mind you – she was well known for kicking off. Nan was fiercely protective and wouldn't back off from anyone. My uncle's wife was also lovely to me, but I can't say the same for my uncle. He lived not far from us, and was known for being a proper nasty bastard, even though he was really short – his nickname was 'Titch'. But his wife could also be real fighter if you pushed her beyond her sweet spot. My uncle actually joined martial-arts lessons to protect himself from her.

To be honest, these days, I think social services would've been all over my case. There was some love there from my parents, but I just think they didn't have a fucking clue about how to raise kids. They needed someone to come in, sit them down and tell them all about how to raise kids.

You might be getting the picture by now that I was surrounded by hard people. In those days, in that place, you had to be. If you were weak, my family would eat you up with chips and a pint on the side. Those who didn't have physical toughness (as in the case of one of my brothers) compensated by being sly. My family truly wouldn't back off from anyone. My uncle's favourite pastime was to go out with his son-in-law, wait for someone to fuck up, then absolutely destroy them. I remember him coming to our hotel one time, his neck gushing claret. He'd been stabbed in the neck with a pencil, which had snapped off inside him. My mum was literally on the kitchen table doing budget surgery with a pair of tweezers, pulling it out. We didn't take him to hospital – there would be police there (the other guy was a lot worse off).

These things were common, daily occurrences. Consequently, the police visited like they were stuck in a revolving door. If my early life were a film, blue lights were the stage lighting and police radios the soundtrack. Given my family's reputation, the police never just visited in ones or twos; we used to have fucking nervous van loads of cops turn up, sometimes for us kids, sometimes for the adults. You look at the way we acted, and from the present it seems like terrible behaviour, but at the time it's just the way kids lived in our part of the world. We considered all of our crimes to be low-level, although now I realise the rest of the world doesn't see it like that. One of my brothers nicked a milk float once – you know, one of those old electric milk floats with hundreds of crated bottles tinkling on the back. He leapt into the driver's seat like a rally pro and went screaming off down the street at a neck-bending twelve miles an hour. These vehicles are the world's simplest vehicles to drive – there are basically just an accelerator, brake and steering wheel – yet he still managed to smash it into a lamp post. So the police came knocking, but one of my other brothers took the blame because he was under the age of prosecution, so nothing came of it. Little did I know it at the time, but watching all this I was basically building up a database of tricks to evade the law.

As much as my parents weren't academically clever, when it came to street-wisdom they were pretty slick. I can remember as teenager getting in violent trouble say, twenty-five miles from home, and ringing my mum to help out. By the time I got home there would be a fresh change of clothes laid out, and all my alibis just as neatly stacked up. If my clothes had blood on them they would be bagged up straight away and sent to another house to be washed or even destroyed. By the time the police arrived I would apparently have been at home all night with twenty witnesses to testify to the fact that I was an absolute angel. It's harder to do that now with cameras, smartphones and all the other shit that tracks us, but back in the day my family were real professionals at staying one step ahead. It also helped that there was so many of us – there was always a different alibi, a different location, a different vehicle.

During my early years, I actually wasn't much of a fighter. This didn't shield me from violence, however. The first major non-family beating I had came when I was eleven years old. Two eighteen-year-olds got hold of me and decided to hammer the fuck out of me – one of my brothers had pissed them off and when they couldn't find him to knock about, they decided I was the next best thing. They got inventive. They picked me up by the ankles and swung me round and round and round, then released me like an Olympic hammer throw into a wall, splitting my head open. This was in a park in broad daylight, with families milling about. They had fucked up big time, however, as now my family would descend on them like those fucking helicopters on the Vietnamese village in *Apocalypse Now*. The police came belting in to grab these two guys, essentially for their own safety. They told them, 'Right, you need to go because his family are coming!' A particularly satisfying memory I have is of seeing the sheer panic on a policeman's face when the vans and cars started screeching up, and all my brothers began piling out with baseball bats and fucking chains, proper tooled up.

Make no mistake, my family were affectively a gang, pit bulls on long chains. They were all big lumps, some of them were even fat fuckers, but together the family could really handle itself. Here's how it worked. My brothers could beat me up, but if someone outside the family had a go at me then they would answer to everyone. Everybody would look out for everybody else in the family. Unfortunately, that would change…

So where was my sister in all this? There was a bit of resentment between us when we were growing up. We were closest in age out of all of the siblings. I used to love seeing her, although I didn't get to spend much time with her because she lived in Essex with her mum. I put her up on a pedestal, idolised her, at least from a distance. But then I fucking hated her when she came to visit. She used to get jealous of what she thought was the close relationship between me and my dad, which it wasn't. He literally walked out on her when she was five years old, and my mum used to force her to visit. My dad would get giddy around her when she was there, like she was a visiting princess, but the minute she had gone he couldn't give a fuck.

Violence was always lurking around every corner, and home was no sanctuary. Take one of my earliest memories, a full-on mash-up between my dad and one of my brothers, who was just fifteen at the time. They were both in the bar of the hotel, after hours. All the usual punters had drifted out and it was just my dad and a few of my brothers left in the bar. This was a dangerous part of the day. As usual my dad had been absolutely tanking-down the drinks – by midnight he was steaming. I was upstairs in my room, in bed. Then I remember my youngest brother came sprinting flat out through the hotel, shouting and screaming, and there was lots of commotion down in the bar. I leapt out of bed and shot downstairs. It took my junior brain a good while to process what was in front of me. I can just remember butcher's-shop levels of blood everywhere, accompanied by lots of flap and panic. In fact, the only person not panicking was my dad, who was sat there cradling a gin and tonic, a drink that was now mixed with the blood pouring down from his smashed head. He still kept drinking this fucking ghastly cocktail. He had a massive slash from the side of his temple down to his eye, the entire side of his head was pushed forward – it looked like someone had tried to skin his face. You could see the back of one of his eyes. My mum is screaming and trying to patch him up. Yet my dad is still mouthing at my brother, saying that he's going to fucking kill him. What happened was that my dad, who was a really mean bastard when drunk, had decided to beat up my youngest brother, Dean. This particular brother had received a kicking in the recent past from dad, and this time he was ready for him. He went for it, hitting my dad in the face with a punch and knocking him backwards into the bar. As Dad fell backwards, my brother went for the finishing move, picking up a heavy barstool by the legs and smashing him across the head with it, busting my dad's head open like a watermelon.

We're talking serious injuries here. My dad was in hospital for just over a year. He had brain surgery and his face reconstructed with metal plates. You can find some humour in bits of this, though. His tear ducts, for example, were rebuilt with glass, and every few years the doctors had to change these ducts – he had a little glass jar in which he kept some of the discarded ducts. He cries a lot from the damaged eye.

The police were involved with this incident, but the official story was that he fell – my brother would've gone to prison if we had taken any other line. I remember that there were lots of congratulations sent to my brother from the legions of other people whom my dad had pissed off. My mum's ex-husband, who was actually a good friend of my dad (he was sniffing around my mum until she died), came in and congratulated my brother, but all my brother said was: 'You're next.' This killed the vibe straight away.

I used to have beatings all the time off my brothers and my old man. One of my brothers in particular, ruthlessly knocked me about, and his mates used to join in to spread to fun. One of the first times I can remember getting properly hurt was by my nan's boyfriend (my dad's mum's boyfriend). I thought he'd broken my arm and he smashed my face off a table. And this was in a 'playfight,' which was actually just an excuse for him to be a vicious cunt. Whenever he really hurt me, he always say, 'Oh sorry, we were just play fighting.' So he used to beat the fuck out of me.

If you are thinking, 'At least he could escape to school.' Think again.

CHAPTER 2 ROCK BOTTOM

I've never been able to discover who said that school days should be 'the happiest days of your life.' Whoever it was must have been a silly little twat. He definitely didn't go through a decade of getting the crap kicked out of him, which was the core of my experience. For me, school days was basically the shit filling in a sandwich between infancy and adulthood. It did me one favour, however – I learned how to fight.

My first proper scrap with someone my own age was in school. There was this one kid, and obviously he had it coming. I don't know what he had done – maybe he was just fat and ugly and in my way – but I remember headbutting him, my forehead going into his face like a cannonball. I can remember that we were grappling, and I was trying to hit him but couldn't get on target. So, I just grabbed him by the hair and levered him down onto my knee, totally caving his nose in. Now bear in mind, this was pre-school – I was like some weird midget MMA fighter. The teachers, obviously, were not impressed and I was thrown out of the school.

I'd obviously picked up a few techniques from watching the grown-ups fight. I also had other less than stellar role models. I was hanging out with one of my older brothers, who was sixteen or seventeen, and he in turn was hanging out with all the docks kids, most of them absolute head cases. They used to play all sorts of weird medieval-type games. We're not talking about jolly days playing tennis in the street or bobbing for apples. One particular source of fun was when two kids would run at each other, then leap into the air and see if they could knee their opponent in the face. It was like something Genghis Kahn and his Mongol hordes would do for fun when they weren't raping and pillaging. Or they would simply grab another guy by his coat hood, pull it down over his head and, again, knee him in the face. (Obviously the gang felt that closing the gap between faces and knees was important.) I can also remember carrying a flick knife for all the, er, knife fights a seven-year-old would get into. Clearly my early world view was a long way from normal.

From the get-go, I hated school with a passion. I was slow – what they call 'learning difficulties' nowadays, but back then we would encouragingly call kids like me 'fucking thick.' In my adult years I've been diagnosed as autistic, but in those grim days you just categorised as the class idiot and written off. The only reason I later got diagnosed was because one of my own kids received the same diagnosis. The child psychologist who was assessing him, and who obviously was checking me out on the sly, basically said to me, 'Do you realise that you're autistic as well?' I shot back, 'How do you know?' She replied, 'Well I've just spent two days talking to you.' It wasn't exactly ego-boosting information, but it did explain a lot about my school years.

Some kids grow up with 'tiger' parents, always encouraging them to excel academically. My parents were not in that camp. I was always told that studying wasn't for us. I don't think my parents came to a single parents' evening during all the years I was in school. That's not fucking normal, although they might simply have been avoiding two hours of teachers telling them their son was a social menace. But there was a lot of other stuff going on at home that meant I wasn't destined to be the brightest bulb at school. We had moved – we'd gone from Grangetown to Sully – so I was surrounded by new, hostile faces. I can remember sitting in class, the clock on the wall grinding out agonising, slow minutes, not being able to do the work, the teacher demonstrating years of professional experience by screaming at me like I was a fucking convict.

I was a mess, admittedly. I've got a photo from those days, and I have no fucking crotch in my trousers, holes in my trainers, and my hair all over the place – yes, I was that kid. I'm surrounded by lots of well-dressed polished little fuckers from some of the affluent catchments, and I'm sat at the end of the line looking like a Dickensian orphan about to be hanged for pickpocketing. There are thirty-two kids in a school photo and I'm the only one not wearing school uniform. I just didn't give a fuck.

But if I got into trouble at school, this was a long way from being in trouble at home. In fact, my family would turn up at the school, and after the teachers told them what violence I had done to another kid, my brothers used to say to me, 'Nice one.' or, 'Good lad.' There were absolutely no repercussions from family, in fact my dad and mum were more likely to tell the teachers to fuck off. So I got to walk away smugly, leaving the teachers fuming, but with my family going, 'That was fucking awesome!' Why wouldn't I hit the next kid whose face got it my way?

Then it happened. Sometimes in life, a truly shattering event occurs, an earthquake that destroys everything and keeps delivering decades of aftershocks. It was 1986. One of my brothers was driving somewhere with his wife and his two children, my niece and nephew, who were aged four and six. I was close to these kids, who were really sweet. My brother and sister-in-law were driving along a motorway at speed in wet conditions. The car suddenly aquaplaned in standing water, skittering from side to side across the carriageways, and my brother couldn't bring the vehicle back under control. The car piled into the central reservation of a motorway overpass, then rode up the slope until it smashed into the supports of a concrete bridge spanning the motorway. It then tumbled back down the slope, and as it did so my six-year-old niece was flung from her seat and out through the windscreen, landing on the road some distance ahead of the vehicle. A passing car stopped, and the driver picked her up off the road and took her to hospital – she died there. My four-year-old nephew, meanwhile, remained trapped in the car and choked to death on his own blood in front of my brother.

Jesus, it was all so fucked up. My brother survived but broke his back in eighteen places and was at death's door. His wife got out of it with just a broken arm. Adding to the sheer futility of the accident, it came out a few years later that she'd actually punched him in the face as they were driving, distracting him just when he needed to focus on the road.

I was just ten years old at the time. I answered the call from another family member, trying to find my mum. This is literally what he said: 'Your brother's had an accident. Rebecca and James are dead. You've got to go and get your mother.' Then he hung up. Who says that to a fucking ten-year-old? They all went off to the hospital, and I got left with a neighbour for two horrible weeks. This was fucking ironic because up to this point my dad used to beat up the neighbour all the time, and now I'm having to live with him. They hated each other, but apparently, in those days, neighbours helped each other when things went wrong, so my dad just said to him, 'Here, take the kid. He's living with you for a bit.'

Living with this stranger is bad enough, but I'm also going to school. Everybody there knows what's happened, so I'm that freak kid. Kids and teachers were being nice to me, but that in a way it was more horrible than when they treated me like a twat. Before the accident, most of the parents at the school wouldn't let their kids talk to me because I was 'that kid' and suddenly you've got all these fuckers trying to be nice to me and seeing if I was alright. Well, where were they before this happened? It was hypocritical as fuck. I can remember thinking, 'You wouldn't talk to me last week, but now my niece and nephew are dead and my brother is dying you're acting like the caring community. Fuck off because I don't want to talk to you now.'

During this time, the grown-ups were also doing all their immature shit, cementing my impression that human beings just aren't that likeable. When I was at the funeral, they were showing due reverence and dignity by all getting pissed. I remember sitting there watching all these people crying, completely steaming. Then the arguments and fights broke out – there was even a punch-up outside the church. I just didn't get it.

To this day the death of those kids breaks me. The accident destroyed fucking everything. My brother was in hospital for a long time, and while he was there the papers were hounding the family, because I think they knew that my sister-in-law had hit her husband. I remember being in the house and these predatory press rats were at the door all the time. My dad got in trouble because he went out and beat one up one of them on the doorstep. We also didn't know if my brother was going to pull through – he did. To make life extra hard, my mum totally lost the plot She believed that she had dreamt of the accident before it happened. As her brain went into absolute meltdown, she convinced herself that she was psychic and she could've warned everyone before the accident happened, so she was blaming herself. It produced a complete mental breakdown. I can remember going home for lunch from school and finding the front door locked. My mum was inside but wouldn't open it to let me in, so I ended up just going back to school and sitting there until a teacher found me and took me to the canteen for some food.

My dad? Well I don't think he gave a fuck really. My brother was in intensive care for a very long time and one of my other brothers, Brandon, had to pick up his business and keep running it. They actually had two offices which they ran separately, although they faced each other with a shared reception. They were operating big companies – I think between them they used to have about seventy employees. Just to layer on the problems that little bit more however, my survivor sister-in-law went predictably mental and then in the midst of this it turned out that she was having an affair while my brother was hovering on the brink of death in hospital. He found out about it because one of my other brothers told him – smart fucking move! After he found out he just wanted to commit suicide, but he was paralysed from the neck down, so unless he could get an evil nurse to smother him with a pillow he was here to stay. So his kids are dead, he's paralysed, he's just found out his wife is having an affair, and now his business is failing. When he eventually came out of hospital his company only lasted another six or seven months. He blamed the other brother for running the business into the ground and so they had a big falling out. He even thought that it was his brother who was fucking his wife while he was in hospital – he wasn't.

All this was too much, and it was basically the end of my family. The sheer bloody trauma, the distrust, the recriminations, all cut the ties between us, as frayed as they were in the first place. I was a pretty lost little boy. I must take my cap off to a Jamaican family who lived next door. They were really lovely and looked after me a lot. They were one of the few stable influences on my early life.

Following all this, life at primary school took the express elevator down to the basement full of shit. I never used to go to school. I didn't bunk off either – my mum just let me stay at home to keep her company after her breakdown, as she was lonely. I used to go into school maybe two days a week, if that. Social Services came round a few times and they were probably told to go and get fucked. But back then it wasn't like nowadays. Today I would've been taken straight into care, but then it was all about keeping families together (or basically ignoring the worsening problems of vulnerable kids, to look at it another way). The school didn't really get involved because they were proper nervous of my family, especially as my dad had by now built up an unchallenged track record of punching headmasters. I think two of my headmasters and one of my brother's headmasters got laid out by my dad. My parents would always march into school on the attack, so teachers would handle them like they were fucking unexploded ordnance.

Looking back, however, when the kids died some of the teachers were really good with me, giving me attention I'd never had before. There was one teacher in particular who was amazing. She taught me mostly in the last year of primary school, and before our family tragedy she was a right fucking witch. Absolutely awful. But I can remember going into her class in the final year and she was a different person. Many years later, when I was an adult, I spoke with her. She said that initially she didn't realise what my home situation was really like, but the death of my relatives brought the full picture into focus for her. Someone was now actually being the responsible adult and standing in my corner. She fought to get me out of all the dummy classes, telling people that I was actually quite a smart kid.

She really was the gift that kept on giving. When I was about to go up to secondary school, she prepped me for that, and by the time I left her class I had friends and what was approaching a relatively normal school life. She spent hours with me, way above and beyond what you'd expect a teacher to do, pulling me out the black pit back into the light. She built me up. I was convinced that I was stupid, but she quickly cottoned on to what was going on at home and realised that this wasn't the case. She took the time to talk to me.

I used to work with her on a one-to-one basis three times a week to bring me on academically. She had her work cut out, because I couldn't read and write properly. When I first went to school I was given my work books, but I wasn't even capable of writing my own name on them. I had this terror of standing up there on my own at the front of the school room, the class pissing themselves laughing at me – the boy who couldn't write his own name. I found a workaround, which was to stand about in the corridor and grab some random kid who could write my name for me. But with this teacher, I used to listen to taped audiobooks, including ancient classics like Homer's *Odyssey*, which I loved. I soaked them up and she was blown away. She used to tell me how proud she was that I was listening to these great books, and I was only ten years old. She really helped me out. I think I learned more in that last year of primary school than I did in my entire secondary education.

In a terrible way, those kids dying was probably helpful for my development in a lot of ways. Suddenly everyone knew what was going on in my family and they started to realise why I was different to other kids. But in the case of the kids, normal fucking service soon resumed. Before long, I was getting beaten senseless at school as well. There was one kid in particular who used to pick on me. He was a little bastard – his family were quite well off – who would take things too far all of the time and hunt me down in the corridors and corners of the school, his pack of jackal mates in tow. A lot of the bullying was verbal – he used to take the piss out my terrible clothes and any other aspect of my appearance he could latch on to. Mentally he used just beat me down and down and down, to the point where I struggled to fight back because he was in my head. I was just too frightened to hit him. So he was all over me, and this went on for about two years. And now the kids had just died, and there was no family about. Mentally, I was here, there and everywhere, a real mess. Here was a little kid who really needed help.

I was not entirely passive with my fists at this time, though. I did get into trouble just after the kids died, when I gashed some kid's face open. It began as a silly kiddy fight – lots of pushing and huffy punches – but I brought some adult shit into the game by grabbing his head and smashing it onto a bookshelf. One of the brackets ripped right up his face. I thought I'd get in trouble for that one, but I was lucky – he was a bit of a tool, and his family were even more scummy than mine. When it came out that he had effectively started it, they let me off.

Then came secondary school. Although it was a new building, new teachers, new classes and new kids, everything continued as normal – I had a fucking terrible time. It was murder, and I had a massive target on my back. I was the scruffy, neglected kid everybody found funny and wanted to fuck about with. There was one particular kid who gave me a really hard time, but eventually I found some balls to take him on. Some US Navy SEALS once wrote on a bunker wall in Afghanistan: *It turns out my dear old mother was wrong, sometimes violence does solve problems.* Well, I started getting this point in the 1980s and '90s. I thought, 'Fuck it!' and I battered the kid, really smashed him up. It began again as a basic playground fight, which he started. For the first few exchanges, it really looked like no one was going to get hurt. I decided that was not on, so I basically hit him with a spinning crescent kick, absolute Bruce Lee masterpiece. My heel caught him on his chin and knocked him clean out. And then, while he was on the floor, I jumped on his head. And then I kicked his head. And then I kept kicking his head. And I stamped on his hands. He went to hospital that day.

Obviously I got into some trouble for this, but it was a pretty indifferent punishment – I was suspended from school for a week. I was also meant to go to evening detention sessions, but my parents decided that I simply wasn't going to attend. They basically said to me, 'If you don't come home at the normal time from school then you're in big trouble.' So I've got the school saying to me, 'You've got an after-school detention,' and at the same time I've got my dad saying to me, 'If you go to that detention I'm gonna fucking hammer you.' My family won out – my headmaster wasn't going to beat the shit out of me, but my dad was, so the decision was easy. Thankfully, the school kind of admitted that the kid deserved a bit of a battering, as he'd pounded me so many times before and got away with it.

You'd thinking hospitalising the lad would have given me the rep to keep others at bay. But now, in fact, I was on everybody's fucking fight radar. The kids in my own year were scared of me, but all of the older, bigger kids fancied having a crack at me, especially as the kid I'd hurt knew a lot of bad people, who swarmed on me like hornets killing a scorpion. It all made me a bit of a marked man and I started to get beaten up more often. I remember one day in particular. A gang of kids attacked me on the school bus. There must've been about nine of them holding me down and hammering the shit out of me. There was no mercy (another thing I've learned about fighting). I staggered off the bus, all torn and bleeding, with a headache and bruises, but I didn't say a word to my parents. Even as I walked into the house I didn't say jack shit to them.

The local landlord's daughter was on the bus. She was a bloody lovely girl; I fancied her so much. Anyway, she went crying to her dad and told him what a hard time I was having at school and that I'd been beaten up on the bus. So he thought he'd mention it to my dad. Hell is paved with good intentions, as they say, and he'd made a big mistake. One night my dad gets home and he's been drinking, which never did anything to improve his character. He comes over to me and looks menacing. 'You got beat up today.' So then I got a hammering from him for being soft. I just couldn't fucking win.

I'm not going to claim that my own childhood years were worse than anyone else's… actually, fuck it, I am. They were absolute murder. Certainly, my own personal levels of violence began to creep up. A high point, or low point, depending on your perspective, was when I was faced with a simple decision – which was worse, getting my head kicked in by a local hard-nut kid or by my dad?

One lovely day, I was on the bus heading home. Then – shit! – a local nutter got on and sat behind me. I could feel his eyes jabbing into the back of my head like a fucking sharp pencil. He absolutely hated me. I knew that the only reason he'd got onto that bus was to give me a massive kicking when I got off.

The bus would stop near my home, outside a local pub. Incidentally, I was sweet on the girl who lived inside the pub, and I used to hang outside optimistically with my mates – what better way to attract the opposite sex than standing on a pavement and acting like a dick? But right now, there were more pressing problems. The bus pulled up.

Time to run.

I knew my terrain. There was this little twisting path called the Snake Path, which ran from the pub to my home. Or, I could take a different route around the crescent back to my house – both were about the same distance. I was gauging whether I could get across the road before this guy grabbed me, and how that played out was going to determine which route I took. And then – shit again! – I saw my dad watching me. He was stood there, across the road. There was absolutely no gentle fatherly instinct in his eyes. In fact, I realised that if I didn't fight this guy, my dad would smack me about even worse, a punishment beating. I was properly caught between a rock and a hard place. Suddenly running wasn't an option.

Fuck it, I'll fight the lad. At least if this guy did start to win, my dad would then step in and thrash him. But my opponent was bigger and stronger than me. Then it came to me, a proper flash of street-thug inspiration. I saw a car coming down the road. Quite instinctively, I just shoved the kid out in front of the car. It smashed into him at about thirty miles an hour with a hell of a bang. He took off like failed Brazilian space launch – the impact flung him off the car back onto the road and pavement. I think he broke both his legs; it's hard for me to remember because my dad was busy extracting me from the scene. Actually, the lad was lucky, because this particular car was going at quite a steady pace, whereas lots of the vehicles (hot hatchbacks, big exhausts, stickers and stripes everywhere – you know the type) came screaming through like they were trying to break the land speed record. Even if it was one of those cars, though, I still would've pushed him in front.

What did my dad think of all this? He bought me a bag of sweets for being a good boy. It was one of the only times he showed that he was proud of me. Different family, eh?

After this, things started to change. People realised that the worm had turned, and they looked at me in a whole different way. Remember, this was my first year of comprehensive school, so I was only about eleven years old. You could see people thinking, 'Hang on, this kid's not fucking right.' A few of the local hard lads still wanted to have a go. But I'd started to bond with a little group of friends, so now I had the force of numbers. I was also getting a bit of a reputation as a nutter. Then, I got an absolute pasting off this kid – I say kid, but he was actually seventeen, way older than me. Supposedly I'd done something to piss him off, but I don't think that was true – he just wanted to batter a kid in my year and take me down at the same time. That's when things really changed because he hammered me. But he fucked-up big time. We used to have this family at the end of our street; they were travellers, and good friends of ours. They got wind of my beating, and the next thing you know their older brothers have turned up to administer justice. These kids were so fucking wild that I remember being properly scared for the kid who had beaten me up – I thought they might kill him. They didn't, quite, but they seriously hurt him. Now everybody in the school realised that you didn't fuck about with me or my mates – that's just how it was.

When it came to the teachers at secondary school, gone was the saintly lady of my primary school years. There was one teacher who was an absolute bastard. He was the worst type of human being ever, an absolute piece of shit. I hated him with a passion. One lunchtime, I was coming out of the sweet shop outside the school gates (we were allowed outside during break times) and he was walking up the street and started having a go at me. Then my sister-in-law comes up, and she knew this teacher. And holy fuck he obviously had a proper boner for her because after he realised the connection he was suddenly my best friend and my advocate all the way through school. He went from being an absolute cunt to treating me as if I was made of gold. I could get away with any shit. If I didn't do my homework he wouldn't bollock me, whereas he would roast other kids alive. People used to take the piss out of me and call me 'Lionel's little bum boy' because I couldn't do anything wrong. It was proper weird, but I wasn't going to complain. Overall though, the teachers and the school were complete shit (it actually has a pretty good reputation today).

As I went into my secondary school years, I started a fight a *lot* more. While all this is going on, my mum is having a mental breakdown and the family is tearing itself apart with grief. You might be thinking, 'This can't get any worse.' Oh but it could – fate decided to hand out all the shit cards at once. Brandon had started to do really well with his own company. He had a fleet of vehicles, shit loads of employees. He approached the rest of the family wanting to borrow money to expand out. What he didn't tell us was that he was about half a million quid in a hole. So the family all borrowed money against their houses, but the money he borrowed still left him £300,000 short of his debts. We are talking 1989, so that was a huge amount of money back then. Anyway, the noose ended up tightening around Brandon's company, and he went under, with my family copping the liability. We ended up losing everything. My parents saw it coming, and luckily they sold their house before it was repossessed. They paid off the money that was borrowed against it and we bought a plot of land and a barn that was falling down not far from Rhyl. But still, all of my family lost an absolute skip-load of money. So I found myself being pulled out of school after I'd been going there for about six months as we relocated up to mid-Wales. Believe you me, this did not bring salvation. But there was a difference – by this time I'd truly discovered the martial arts.

CHAPTER 3 HITTING THE MAT

Okay, by now you are probably thinking, 'This kid is doing a hundred miles an hour down the track and all the wheels are starting to lift off.' You aren't far wrong, but one of the things that kept me from going full fucking mental around this time was the fact that I was doing a ton of martial arts. I couldn't see it at the time, but the martial arts would play an absolutely central role in the life ahead of me, giving me a centre nothing else provided.

If it involves punching, kicking, grappling and generally smashing people in the face, I've done it all – karate (most styles), wrestling, Muay Thai, kickboxing, boxing, to name a few. Nor is this just Saturday morning dabbling. I got my first black belt in karate by the time I was seventeen and would eventually rise to fifth *dan* black belt years later. I've fought in more national and international competitions than I can count and trained literally hundreds of students of all ages, from infants to grandparents, guiding many of them to black-belt standard and beyond. My martial arts skills have taken me into the movies, both on the screen (usually as a nasty bastard villain), stuntman or stunt coordinator, and in training actors who need to kick ass with more than just a beer-hall haymaker. In addition, although it might be hard to see, martial arts have helped give me the grit and discipline to get back to my feet, however many times life has slammed me to the mat.

Like a lot of adrenaline-jacked kids of the 1980s, I bought into the whole high-kicking mythology of the martial arts, courtesy of TV and film. I was obsessed with *Enter the Dragon* and Bruce Lee's apparent invincibility, with his blistering one-inch punch and bullwhip-fast kicks. (Only later did his whooping noises come across as, well, a bit fucking weird.) In 1984 *Karate Kid* the movie was released, and it seemed like the whole world went ninja. Apparently, all it took was polishing a car and wearing a bandana to achieve lethal fists and triumph over one's enemies. Looking back at that film, the 'Kid' character – Daniel LaRusso – couldn't fight boredom let alone the psychos who lived around me, but we were taken in. We all wanted to be on that path to fighting enlightenment.

My early education in the martial arts came from the screen. That wasn't the only thing I learned from TV. Given the lax parental oversight, there was no age restriction on what I watched – violence and porn were all there, full frontal, so people's faces weren't the only thing I saw getting roughly handled with fists. Moving quickly on… I didn't start my journey into the martial arts through classes, even though there were lots of them around. Instead, I pursued a rough and ready 'self-education' – i.e. imitating on-screen martial artists by acting insane and smashing up my own home – this was when I was about five or six.

The TV and film heroes weren't my only inspiration to begin martial arts training. The other fuel was that my brothers simply liked to fight, and I desperately needed some techniques so I could hold my own. (Incidentally, one of my brothers could've been an amazing boxer, but they couldn't find a glove big enough for his head – he was always headbutting people.) Anyway, I began boxing a bit with the boys, learning some crude but surprisingly effective fundamentals about jabs, crosses, hooks and uppercuts. Boxing has stayed with me regardless of what martial arts I've pursued – it's a true king of fighting sports. Plus, I've always loved the cocky expression of some competition fighter who thinks he's king of the hill right up to the moment you almost decapitate him with a right hook, after which he just lays there on the mat twitching like a freshly landed fish. It's always been worth the disqualification.

A big change came when we had this guy called Paul move into the hotel. He came with some emotional baggage – his parents had kicked him out because basically he was really fucking odd. I can remember him looking huge when I was little, but from an adult perspective he was a right oompa loompa – he was 5ft 3in tall. But he was a massive ball of energy. Paul was heavily into martial arts, mainly karate and kung fu. Alongside the hotel, we had quite a big garden with a Portakabin at the end of it, and this became a den of iniquity for me, my teenage brothers and all our mates. I used to go down there with Paul, and he would train me up, mostly in Wing Chun kung fu, with a bit of Lau Gar thrown in, and then eventually some karate. We would also train with swords, bats, knives and other stuff – how I didn't bleed to death in that Portakabin I do not know. At the same time, I decided to get into running. By the time I was about ten years old, I virtually became South Wales's version of the *Roadrunner* cartoon. I used to run a circuit from my house down to the coast and back, which was about 15 miles distance, and I'd do that several times a week. I was super fit.

But watching unrealistic movies and training with a tiny man in a hut could only take me so far, and I eventually joined a Kyokushinkai karate club. That didn't last long – the days and times didn't work out – so I moved to a Wado Ryu karate club at a YMCA in *B*—. Although the club was Wado Ryu, and thus carried long traditions of techniques, it actually belonged to one of the country's first freestyle associations. This essentially means that, to a degree, anything goes, so basically I was learning freestyle kickboxing under a really exceptional teacher. I had found my calling.

Apparently I was quite good at the techniques and I progressed through the belts pretty quickly. I also had the advantage that I was super flexible, like a fucking proper Stretch Armstrong doll. By the time I went to that class, I had already been training for about two or three years – *daily*. And when I wasn't down in the Portakabin or in the garden with Paul, I was dicking about in the house, doing my level best to kick people in the head. One misguided but useful exercise I'd been doing was attempting to kick flies circling around a ceiling lamp. It was the world's shittest strategy for insect control, but as a by-product I'd built up impressive flexibility.

It soon became time for my first major competition, held in that jewel of southern England, Swindon. In the past I had done a few minor competitions under the umbrella of the Amateur Martial Association (AMA), and I'd picked up a couple of medals when I was about eight. But this was my first step into the proper competitive world of martial arts. I was now a warrior destined for battle, not some goofy kid trying to survive life.

When you watch martial arts competitions in the United States, all the competitors are there in expensive, matching, competition jackets, travelling in an air-conditioned super-bus to an elite stadium, cheered by crowds of 20,000 people while TV commentators narrate every move. Bit different in South Wales in the late 1980s. They picked me up from my house in the fucking drizzle with the whole squad piled into the back of a builder's transit van. We couldn't afford anything posh like a minibus with actual seating, so we just rolled about in the windowless cabin like loose timber. We also had to stop the van on the way to the venue because the guy who was driving had been smoking a spliff and the van was so full of smoke that the entire squad was getting high.

As you might have gathered, I wasn't a member of a *nice* club. All the guys were pretty much local hard nuts, just as used to street brawls as competitive martial arts. I was also the youngster of the club – all the rest were either grown men or kids in their late teens – so I had to toughen up at a sprint. Unlike most other martial arts clubs, we also didn't touch *kata* in the club for the first three belts. A quick definition of terms is needed here: *Kata* is basically choreographed sequences of martial arts movements, designed to develop physical coordination, power, mental control and fighting spirit. Although the *kata* are performed solo against an imaginary opponent. Each move is meant to represent an element of a real fight and should be performed accordingly. I do not decry *kata*, but it can be a bit of a refuge for those who don't want to get hurt. In our club, therefore, the emphasis was all on *kumite*, which is basically sparring with a partner. 'Sparring' means different things to different people. To some, *kumite* means light contact and fast moves, oriented towards scoring competition points. In our club it meant quite simply that if you didn't block or avoid an incoming blow, you were going to get hurt. The training was as much about taking pain as giving it out, but by consequence we weren't afraid of anyone.

I remember arriving at this competition and thinking 'Fuck!' There were people everywhere. Lots of them had Stars & Stripes *gi*s (a *gi* is a martial arts training suit), so they really looked the part. By contrast, I had my arse hanging out of my thin and torn combat trousers. There was this girl in our squad. She must've been seventeen and had a proper mullet haircut, the type you would see on a prisoner not a teenage girl. She was massively rough – just looking at her you could tell that she was destined to have about fifteen kids with seventeen dads. But she had a wise head on those oblong shoulders and gave me a life lesson. She got hold of me and said, 'It doesn't matter what you're wearing, you just hit harder than all these other fuckers. Just don't fucking lose!'

Well, I didn't. I remember having my first fight and winning it really easily. And I kept winning. Despite it being a fucking big competition, I think I got through six rounds into the final. I remember the fight well. The nerves kicking in. The lights heating up the mat. The noise of the crowd, baying for at least some blood. The fight itself didn't exactly go to plan. I was moving around, throwing out some techniques and looking for my moment to strike. But the annoying cunt opposite kept treading on my extended shin guard pad – we had to wear pads during the fights at that time. This happened several times until he eventually broke the elastic on the shin guard, after which it started flapping about and making me look like a penguin with a limp. So I lost self-control, ran across the mat and headbutted him. The judges were less than impressed, and I got a warning. The fight resumed, but by then I couldn't give a shit about fair play, so I hoofed him in the bollocks and got disqualified. But I still got my third-place trophy. I can remember thinking, 'I got a trophy for kicking someone in the balls.'

I went back home after the competition and my mum and several others saw the trophy. We didn't have mobile phones back in those days, so I couldn't let her know straight away that I'd won. I had actually called her from a phone box from the competition venue to let her know that I was in the final, but I didn't have enough money after the match to let her know how I had done. So by the time I got home, the whole fucking family was there, waiting, and as I walked in with a big trophy they let out a massive cheer. They were all chucking me tenners – I think I got about three hundred quid in total. It was nuts, and a big moment for me. If I had won a trophy for rugby or football, only one or two of them would've been marginally interested and the rest wouldn't have given a shit. But the fact was that I'd won this trophy for *fighting*, and they all bloody loved that. 'He's beat someone up and got a medal. That's fucking great!'

The competition was a big turning point for me, even though I was still only 6th *kyu*. (The belts run from 9th *kyu* for a beginner's first grading through to 1st *kyu*, after which the martial artist can go for his *dan* grade, or black belt.) At that point everything changed in my training as well. It suddenly became serious. I had this flash of philanthropic understanding: 'I can hurt people better using this. There's a whole new bunch of shit I can do to people.' I remember getting a bit more arrogant, walking with a bit more swagger. I went on to win a few more competitions after that.

In terms of the styles of martial arts, I was starting to develop my own ideas and preferences. I had liked the full-contact Kyokushinkai club, but it was a bit too traditional for my freewheeling instincts. The Wado Ryu club suited me down to the ground. You'd walk in and there would be a short warm-up – you'd run up and down the hall about ten times, do the splits, jump up and down, knock out a few sit-ups. Then it was 'Pads on, gloves on, let's go, fight!' You would beat the crap out of each other for an hour. It was absolutely fucking brilliant. Why bother going anywhere else? The instructors brought with them their own distinct flavour and insights. Some of them would disappear for about six months to spend time in one of Her Majesty's Prison and Probation Service institutions, and come back with tales, scars and new fighting tips. It was that sort of club.

Some more delicate readers (if you are one, seriously, why are you reading this?) might see this type of martial arts training as basically an apprenticeship for young thugs. But this is missing the point. The martial arts can be a real gift to give to kids, especially to those without guidance or structure in their lives outside the *dojo* (the room or hall in which instruction takes place). I've taught hundreds of kids myself, and it brings almost nothing but benefits. The first thing it gives them is discipline. For me, martial arts taught me that whatever happens, good and bad, is a direct consequence of my actions. The *dojo* also showed me that there is an easy way and a hard way to do things, or to put it another way, a wrong way and a right way. Which route you take is down to you, but the martial arts, if done well, teach you to confront and to dominate the hard path, no matter how much it scares you.

The main thing the martial arts have taught me is to deal with your own shit. We control very little in life, so you've got to control everything that is in your power to do so, while facing your fears and learning from your own mistakes. For example, I would later run a successful security company (I'll tell you more about that in the next book), but the actions of someone else put me out of business. Lessons were learned – and as a consequence, I will never rely on one source of income again, because I put my all into that company and I lost it. I also learned not to trust everything into other people's hands. When I was running my company, I trusted another person implicitly and they betrayed me. I won't make that mistake again. The martial arts, by contrast, was something that I could control in my life, at times when I had very little control over what was happening around me and to me. I could choose to put the training in, or not. I could control my body, or not. I could even control my opponent, or not. The choice rested simply in my hands.

The *dojo* was essentially the world in miniature, forcing me to confront life head on. Even through personal tragedy, violence, family disintegration, moving homes, demolished financial fortunes and more, the *dojo* gave me a place where I could focus and belong. Martial arts are also good equalisers. It doesn't matter who you are, it doesn't matter what you are wearing, or where are you come from. When you're up there on the mat or in the ring (or scrapping it out with bare knuckles on a piece of rough land between hay bales – again, more for future books), all that matters is how you can handle yourself and how hard you are prepared to dig into the fight. I could pay a thousand pounds or twenty quid for a *gi* – whichever one I choose is not going to affect the outcome. My technique and my fighting spirit are the ultimate deciders.

One of things that can freak regular people out about me, I think, is that I almost feel at home in a fight. I even go into a sort of calm state. I think it's partly because fighting is so very *honest*. When you have a scrap, there's none of the bullshit and complexity like we find in the rest of the world. One of the reasons why I later backed off doing a lot of karate competitions was that they are not *real*, at least not in my way of thinking. I started to get disqualified from competitions on a regular basis. Onlookers could always tell when I was about to get officially booted off the mat because I'd go from an orthodox karate stance to some kind of predatory boxer's guard, just before I absolutely fucking lamped my opponent. What used to really rile me up was when I would score a point, but it wouldn't get counted by the judges because it wasn't pretty enough. Then all of a sudden my opponent would score on me with a really snappy looking technique and a sharp *kiai* scream, but I knew that technique wouldn't be effective in real life. So that's when I would think, fuck it, I'm going to show you what proper technique looks like. Bang!

The thing is, I really didn't care. I still don't. To me it wasn't about the medals, it was about knocking people out, because in my strange world, that was good honest fun. Hunting for the next dose of realism, I did start training in Muay Thai when I was about seventeen. That was great because it was so fucking brutal, with elbows and knees coming into play, and hacking leg kicks that turned your opponent's leg into a numbed block of plasticine. My training around this time faced an extra challenge, however. I broke my pelvis when I fell into a garage vehicle inspection pit, like a proper clumsy fuck. My dreams of warrior greatness were forcibly put on hold, as I was in traction for about six months and out of action from the fight game for about a year. At least I spent my time wisely, flirting with nurses. When I came back to fitness, I was all revved up to get back in the game. I trained like a nutter for six weeks, entered the British National karate championships, and came in the last six in *kumite*.

Of course, I still had to keep up my stop/start involvement in formal education – it couldn't all be training, scrapping and getting thrown out of competitions. Here was a bit of a grey area. I actually stayed in school until I was eighteen because I hadn't accomplished anything when I was sixteen. I didn't do any GCSEs (the UK's main qualification when kids are sixteen – most kids get about 7–10 of these), although I did get a bunch of Certificates of Education. I actually got six of those with distinction, which really pissed off some of my teachers. Although most of them had decided that I was an illiterate idiot, there was one teacher who saw in me a little sputtering flame of intelligence. He felt that I could probably do quite well if I put my mind to it. However, I pretty much told him to get fucked because I didn't want to put in the effort. And when I got the results he said to me, 'These could be As in GCSEs, you're a fucking idiot.' I'm like, 'Fine, I'm a fucking idiot then. Where's the next fight?' There was no talking to me. Youth is, as they say, wasted on the young.

The basic idea of my education between sixteen and eighteen was that I was going to do some sort of diploma, which was essentially like the thick kids' version of sixth form (the last two years of secondary school). I had some extra motivation to stay in school – my parents would receive money from the government if one of the children was still in full-time education. So I remained in education, technically, but I really didn't turn up very much. I'd go in, register myself, and then fuck off down to the bottom of the hill where there was a good café. I had an on/off girlfriend at this time, and her mum used to run this café. So I'd go in every morning with three of my mates and we'd all have a full English breakfast and a cup of tea for about two quid each. Then we'd just hang about chatting for a bit. Diligently avoiding anything that looked like learning, we would next go up to the sports centre for the day and do weights, box each other, play rugby, whatever we fancied. We got on really well with the guy who ran the weights suite, so we'd pretty much train there every day. The school knew exactly what we were doing, but as usual they didn't give a shit – letting me stay away put some distance between them and my headmaster-beating family. We would re-attend school every lunchtime because I got free school meals, and then after lunch it was time to bunk off again. If we did stay in school, we certainly wouldn't dream of attending lessons or anything.

In terms of my future plans, my vague ambitions were either to: a) open a full-time *dojo* or, b) to go into the armed forces. But generally I didn't think about the future too much. I had reached a kind of shitty form of Buddhist enlightenment, focusing on dicking about in the moment. I was enjoying the fact that I was just going out with my mates on the piss, I wasn't in school very much, and I was doing lots of training. I'd have breakfast, head to the gym, run through some *kata*, do some pad training, lift some weights. I'd also play rugby for the school occasionally.

I also had a bit of a name for myself around school, so I could get away with fucking murder if I wanted to. The teachers didn't bother me, because if one of them got on my case I'd simply phone my parents and they'd come down and kick off. They would back me up 100 per cent, saying that I hadn't done whatever I was accused of, even if it was obvious to everybody that I had. One incident springs to mind: I'd had a fight with a kid in my class. He was a right prick, he'd given me a bit of a dig, and I'd sorted him out. He wasn't much of a fighter, but he was an epic gob-shite. We were actually in the playground and he suddenly pulled out a scalpel he'd nicked from the biology classroom, and tried to slash me with it. I quickly clocked the glinting, ultra-sharp steel. As he came at me with the blade I swung my school bag in front of me as a rudimentary shield, and he slashed right down the fabric of the bag – that could have been my torso. This action gave me an opening, however, so I hit him with the power of a fucking metal press. That scared him off for now, and we separated. But he came back later with a tennis racket and started battering me with that in a classroom. He hit me about seven or eight times – I had stripy welts all down the side of my body. I'd had enough. I went into full berserker mode and absolutely pounded him with my fists, then worked him over with the business end of a classroom stool, and then gave him some more with my fists and feet as he lay trembling on the ground. I proper hurt him, so because official school policy frowned on children receiving serious injuries, the teachers got involved.

Here's where my parents again worked their threatening magic. They descended on the school like vengeful Valkyries from the heavens. They dominated the teachers so skilfully that the upshot of the whole incident was the school ended up apologising to me, even though looking back I'd actually been a bit of a prick who could have de-escalated things easily. Sometimes it was like I was wearing a white jacket, but we were telling the school that it was black, and they were accepting it because they were shit scared of the alternatives. That was pretty much the way my dad dealt with the school. I also think that the school gave up on me just because they saw where I had come from, and knew I was beyond their reach.

My non-attendance at school is probably giving you the impression that I was an undisciplined waster. But outside school, things couldn't be more different. Again, martial arts provided a discipline and framework for my life that I couldn't find elsewhere. So when I was sixteen I opened my own karate club in T—. Now this might seem a little bit overconfident for a sixteen-year-old who spent his daylight hours avoiding education and punching people in the face. But by now I had a *dan* grade in Wado Ryu and I had also just recently received a *dan* grade in Shotokan karate.

My two black-belt gradings were totally different experiences. The Wado grading had actually been really informal. Although the Wado governing association was okay, it wasn't as professional as the Karate Union of Great Britain (KUGB). Even the *dan* grades were graded as part of a regular class, rather than going away to a special event. So there was no real ceremony about it – I just knew that I had to knock seven bells out of my opponent to get the grade, which I did happily. We also used to do a lot of pad work in Wado, and if you couldn't whack the pads convincingly enough then you couldn't do the grade. They'd like to see that you had power behind the techniques, which is an area I think the KUGB fails a bit.

Taking my *dan* grade with the KUGB was a totally different kettle of fish. We had to travel to Bath, where I'd be graded by the great karate *sensei* Keinosuke Enoeda. This guy was a global legend. Born in 1935 in Japan, he took up karate under the Japan Karate Association (JKA) during his university years and carved out a formidable reputation, winning the All-Japan Championship in 1963. In 1965 he came over to the UK on what was effectively a karate instructor exchange scheme, but ended up staying and rising to become a fearsome and respected 8th *dan* master and Chief Instructor of the KUGB. He was as hard as a polished anvil (although an absolute gent outside the *dojo*) and his nickname was the 'Tiger'. You did not fuck about when you were to go in front of Enoeda. I'm not entirely sure I got that message.

I was really sick on the morning of the grading. I felt as rough as sandpapered bollocks, and I was physically sick in the car on the way over. From memory, I don't think that I had a hangover, but it couldn't be out of the question. I was also a pretty nervous, because I was getting a lot of hate at the time of the grading. The instructors from one of my old karate clubs were there, and there weren't exactly on my side – I'd had a fight with one of them around town during the lead up to the grading. Looking back, this uneventful scrap was fucking ridiculous. The particular instructor in question was in his twenties and decided to show his maturity by having a fight with me, a sixteen-year-old, outside a pub in Rhyl.

The origins of the fight lay in the fact that we had done a team event in the Welsh National Championships – the team consisting of me and a couple of mates. It should be noted that this was a Senior Men's Team event, and at sixteen there was no way I could be classified as senior anything. Then again, different times. No one seemed to give a fuck – they often let kids into the senior events because otherwise they wouldn't have enough people to fight. Anyway, I had a match against this instructor and he fucking banjo'd me after the referee had called *yamae* (stop). He completely sparked me out. I was stretchered off in front of crowds of people. I didn't give a crap about the actual blow, but what really hurt was my severely bruised pride.

Obviously all this was thumping away inside my brain like a psycho's fist against a wall. A few days later I saw this guy in a seafront pub in Rhyl and I started having a go at him verbally. I got proper territorial and told him he had to leave the pub because this was where I drank with my friends. (Yes I know, I'm sixteen and I'm knocking down pints in the pub – it was no problem back then and no one gave a shit about IDing young people. Good times.) We'd had some strong words before because we used to call him, 'paedo' – his fucking girlfriend was younger than me, it was proper dodgy. I was being gobby, but really wanted to avoid a fight because the pub bouncers were my mates – I didn't want to put them in the awkward position of having to ask me to leave. But like adding more and more items onto the *Buckaroo* mule, our argument was beginning to load up with tension. I opted for a classy move. I picked up his pint, theatrically hacked up a massive blob of phlegm, then spat it into his drink, adding a *Masterchef* touch by stirring it around my finger. 'Right, now what the fuck are you gonna do?' I asked him.

Not much, as it turned out. His spoiled pint led to a bit of pushing and shoving, a bit of nonsense, but it wasn't a proper scrap. But as you might grasp, there was a bit of club rivalry to say the least. They didn't like me at all. It wasn't helped by the fact that I ended up battering in a few of their students at school. They used to talk a lot, but they never really did anything. I was different. I'd just walk up to them smack them one. I was a little cunt basically. But when it came to the actual grading after the training session, I remember doing really well in the *kumite*. I caught my opponent with a couple of really good *mawashi-geri* (roundhouse kicks) to the head. You know they are good when everyone in the room can clearly hear the slap of your foot against the side of his face. I also swept him and put him on his arse. Enoeda was pretty happy with that, nodding wisely and approvingly from his table. I got the coveted *dan* grade from this great figure.

After all this, I found the balls and bravado to set up my own karate club in T—. There was another club in the village, but, without pumping myself up, I was much better than the other instructor. I was training around this time in a town club and also at a local university club, so I knew all the senior trainers at this point. I felt that I had learned enough from them to do it myself. I'd also built up a bit of a reputation around town – I was still getting into a lot of scraps, so people knew who I was and that when it came it fighting, I would teach them the hard stuff. In our area, this reputation did all its own marketing for me. People were queuing up to train with me.

So I opened the class at sixteen. I wanted to place myself under the KUGB umbrella, but given my age I knew I had to play things a bit different. I didn't inform the KUGB straight away, even though I quickly gathered about thirty-five students. I stole lots of them from another local club, led by a guy called Reg S. I'm keeping this twat's name anonymous, but he was a real shyster. He was corrupt, devious and untrustworthy, plus he wasn't good at his martial art. For a time I was actually one of his students, but his class was very *kata* based. I quickly found that I was better than most of them when it came to *kumite*. I even ended up leading *kumite* sessions on occasions. I used to think it was because Reg felt I was a sound student and he could trust me running some sessions. Looking back on it, however, I think he just didn't know what he was doing. All this, plus my dissatisfaction with Reg as a basic human being, fed into my setting up the breakaway club.

I had to solve the KUGB accreditation problem. After about a couple of weeks of running my new club, I got all my students to write letters addressed to the KUGB, basically saying that Reg S. was a cunt and if they couldn't train with me then they wouldn't do karate. Sticking my neck out even more, I turned up at a KUGB annual general meeting with this big pack of letters and whacked them all down on the table. I said to the leaders that I'd opened the club, despite knowing that I shouldn't have, but they could either have all these members with the KUGB or I could fuck off elsewhere and take them with me. There was lots of head-shaking and giggling, not least because I was doing this right in front of Reg S., who was actually in the room staring in wide-eyed disbelief at a sixteen-year-old starting a coup. I had strong backing from some very senior figures, who also disliked Reg S. intensely. One of them, a legendary figure in British karate, called an emergency meeting of the technical committee to see if I could get away with it. Much to Reg's disgust, they gave me the green light. However, I wasn't allowed to be the official *sensei* because I wasn't eighteen yet. So I was the instructor, but my dad was in charge of the affiliation as the designated grown-up. What made it really funny was that one of my teachers used to come and train with me.

The responsibility of running a karate club didn't exactly make me a bastion of moral responsibility. Truth be told, when I was with my karate gang about town, we were always the naughty ones. The core of our club was essentially a right bunch of dodgy bastards. Let's pick some at random: One of the guys was called Nick. We used to call him the 'transport manager', because every time he needed to go somewhere he'd just nick a different fucking car. He was a little fella, but he used to train at a boxing gym with a world champion, so he was handy with his fists. He was, in many ways, a proper little bastard, but he ended up being one of the core members of my club. There was another guy called Jeff. Looking back he was also a right dick. He used to do a ton of drugs, never went to school, and was essentially out on the piss and scrapping all the time. A local mechanic, Bob, also used to train with us. You could pick him out a mile off because he was the only one who would turn up to a karate grading wearing a cowboy hat, in fucking mid-Wales. He also had a massive handlebar moustache; he looked like a Greek football referee acting in a Spaghetti Western. We had new reprobates added all the time. One of my parents' friends used to have lots of foster kids, so every few weeks we would get a fresh set of wrong 'uns coming to train with us. Collectively, I think me and my karate club used to scare the shit out of the locals.

When they were training hard, however, they didn't seem to get into as much trouble. Nick ended up getting arrested for a couple of burglaries, and I wasn't happy about that. Him and Jeff also nicked a Sierra Cosworth and drove it from *T—* to Cardiff. The police clocked them, resulting in a blistering twenty-five-minute car chase around Cardiff, all blue lights and scorched tyres. They both got caught. Mark had a load of bite marks on the back of his leg where the police canine brought him down. Looking back, to me all these jaunts seem quite harmless, but we did get in a lot of trouble and I did like to fight. But at the same time I had a lot of young kids in my karate class and it was all very respectful. Even the most criminally inclined members of the group behaved themselves when they were in the *dojo*. If we were in a pub and someone kicked off, that was a different matter. It was a really weird, mixed bag of people, but we got very close as a group.

As I mentioned before, my mum's house was the first destination you went to after you'd done something bad and needed to cover your tracks. Whatever you did, you made a beeline for 'mam' straight away – everybody called her that. As soon as you arrived at her house, your clothes were off and straight into the washing machine. Then a shower, a fresh change of clothes and, hey presto! you'd been here all day. This practice came in very, very useful with my karate boys. One of the lads got accused of a burglary, for example (which he actually did) and the police were chasing him. He went straight round to my mum's, changed clothes, and then my brothers stuffed him into the boot of my dad's car. They drove him down as far as Lampeter, at which point he transferred into the backseat. Then they took him down to Llanelli, where he stayed at my brother's house for a few days. The police come looking for him round at our house, sensing our involvement. Of course, 'He's not here and he's never been here.' We just tell them that he's been working all week for my brother down in Llanelli. So the police investigate in Llanelli and there he is, just as we said, all scrubbed up and looking like a model citizen. They ask him: 'Where have you been all week?' And, of course, he corroborates my mum and dad's story by saying that he's been down here all week on the building site.

It's one thing to be good at karate. It's another thing entirely to be good at teaching it. Plenty of sixteen-year-olds I know would struggle to find their way out of a room, let alone find the authority to lead thirty-five students in weekly training sessions. I'd acquired a bit of teaching experience previously, helping out with sessions at the university and some other clubs, so I had the self-belief that I could do it. But the thing that gave me the most confidence was simply that I knew my subject. On the topic of how to fight, I was on top of my game. I think anyone can teach, if you know your subject well enough. This confidence meant I wasn't really concerned about standing up in front of people and leading them in a session.

My relationship with the authorities of the karate world was a bit roller-coaster one, however. One time, for example, I was in trouble with the head of a major regional karate squad when I turned up late for training because someone had hit me over the head with a bottle and I had to have my scalp stitched up. Another time I ended up at the very top of the cunt list after getting into trouble up in Blackpool. A very senior figure in the world of karate used to run a course up in Blackpool – England's shit, cold and wet budget version of Las Vegas. I took my merry little band up there to do a grading and some training with the instructor. On Day One we were really well-behaved, all squeaky-clean *gi*s and respectful behaviour. On Day Two, the wheels came completely off and we all went out into Blackpool and got absolutely hammered. I subsequently went rolling around the campsite where we were staying, pissed off my face, and ended up getting into a fight with the security. One of the more elderly karate students decided to intervene and had to pull me away with his walking stick, hooking me around the neck like a shepherd would do to some thick-headed ram trying to fuck a ewe in the next field. Yet many of the more senior KUGB officials seemed to like me, even though half the time they were shaking their heads in despair.

As you can see, having my own karate club did not mean that I stayed out of trouble. Rather it meant that that if I did get into problems, I had an entire gang on my side. And truth be told, a lot of my students were fucking idiots, so we ended up in all sorts of scrapes. For example, a few of the lads got into trouble with a gang of local hard nuts. As a result, I was dragged into the whole mess, after I had a stand-up row in town with one of these gang members. I think I might have even beaten one of them up – it's all a bit of a blur now. Anyway, it developed into a real *us and them* situation. There was honour at stake.

It transpired that one day I spotted a rival guy outside the local train station. He also saw me and started to do the whole peacock-in-heat chest-pumping and neck-pecking thing. He stormed over to me and started to mouth off right in my face. Some people have to talk themselves up to the right moment to start a fight, winding up like one of those old Evel Knievel stunt bike toys. I, by contrast, just mash the accelerator into the floor and smash people in the face as the very first move. I think it's my way of following Mike Tyson's famous observation: 'Everyone's got a plan until you punch them in the face.' Anyway, on this particular occasion I just wasn't in the mood for nuanced chat, so I simply grabbed him by the collar and rammed my forehead into his face – popped him, game over. I walked off and didn't think anything else of it.

All I had done was add more fuel on the bonfire, of course. About a week later, I was waiting for a bus outside the same train station, when about four or five of the enemy gang suddenly appeared and tried to rush me, intent on giving me a group retribution beating. What they didn't realise was, that I was waiting there with the rest of my class, so I had my own personal army as back-up. For a moment, it seemed like there would be a minor civil war, but it ended up with a lot of pushing and shoving and waving handbags. Sometimes fights are like that, more posturing than scrapping. It was fucking stupid. So again, we separated and I went about life.

It still wasn't over, though. A week later, I was on my own, heading over to see my dad, and a big gang of them spotted me. They quickly had me cornered, with nowhere for me to run. Okay, now it was on. There were five of them, and one of them had a chunky looking Staffordshire bull terrier, egging it on to take a chunk out of me. Some of them had also tooled up for the occasion. One of them had a length of chain and another had, well I don't know what it was, it looked like a fucking dildo. Great, my obituary would say I was battered to death with a sex toy while having my leg humped by a dog.

If you are attacked by a gang, you have to seize the initiative from the start, take the wind out of them. As they were winding up for the attack, I grabbed the leader by the throat and told him that if they didn't fuck off I would batter them all. Straight away they knew this wasn't going to be walkover. The leader's response was to tell me that his dog would savage me. So, in response, I grabbed the dog from the floor, lifting it up by its brass collar, and I sank my teeth into its ear – I really bit it. The dog started yelping, its ear pissing with blood. I released the grip with my teeth and threw the dog at its owner's head. The dog tried to grip onto its owner and in so doing actually clawed the hell out of his face. I then grabbed the guy by the throat and screamed in his face, 'I'll eat your fucking dog!' I reinforced the point by turning sharply and punching one of the other members of the gang square in the face. After that, all their gumption left them and they fucked off pretty sharply.

In retrospect, it wasn't my finest hour, because I really love dogs – I feel guiltier about this then any of the human pieces of shit I've beaten up in my life. Furthermore, some passers-by had seen all this and they were pretty freaked out. Talk of the incident went rippling out throughout town, further cementing my reputation as a headcase.

If you live in a violent world, the fact is that is that you are going to take plenty of beatings as well as dishing them out. The gang did get their own back a couple of months later. They took me when I was absolutely pissed. Two of them were across the road from me mouthing off. Wobbling like a new-born foal, with gallons of beer sloshing around inside me like an underfilled fuel tanker, I decided I was going to get them. I'd had my evening kebab after all, and now it was time to complete the great British night out with a good punch-up. I started the pursuit, but it all got a bit comical. I ended up herding them around a car, like when Scooby-Doo was being chased around a table by a ghost, and I just couldn't get to them. What they did achieve, however, was to keep my attention. So while all this was happening, another guy sneaked up on me from behind with a half full bottle of Newcastle Brown ale, and he just smashed me over the back of the head with it.

The sensation was bizarre – it was like the TV channel in my brain suddenly changed. I'd seen these two guys and I was ready to go, but the next thing my mate was sitting in front of me saying, 'Are you alright?'

'Yeah, I'm fine,' I replied, but then and I looked down and there was blood pooling everywhere. I was told that this guy had twatted me with the bottle, then turned and ran along an alleyway down the side of the train station into a park. Apparently, I chased after them for a little bit, but as I got inside the park gates my legs folded beneath me and I went down, I was out cold. Then I got back up, staggered back to the train station and my mates. Fucking funny though. Just another day.

CHAPTER 4 STREET LESSONS

I'll be honest – I would rather fight a second *dan* karate belt than a crackhead who has never done a day's combat training in his life. Why? Because in most cases the martial artist will not only fight *fair*, he also won't know how to really *hurt* people, unless he has trained in a rock-hard fighting club. Instead, he is likely to pull his punches, even if he isn't aware he is doing so, and also to believe that a single hit on his opponent will win the fight. (Believe me, I've smashed some big guys in the face with everything I've got, and they just wobble a bit then come back fighting.) The crackhead, by contrast, is likely to have had dozens of street scraps and will know lots of the dirtiest tricks to *win* at all costs. He is also likely to be mental enough to chew your face off in the fight.

People ask me all the time about the difference between martial arts and street fighting, or how to make the martial arts work in the street. I understand why they might be worried. Some people have spent their whole lives training in martial arts or combat sports, and have never had a proper balls-to-the-wall fight. When they do, they are often demolished by someone with a fraction of the training, or no training at all, but who has tons of street experience. The real fight has none of the choreography built into many *dojo* sparring sessions. All the attacks are delivered with maximum force and no techniques or weapons (improvised or otherwise) are off the table. Crucially, your opponent won't show you any mercy. You can't tap out or take a break in a real fight. Add a potentially paralysing rush of adrenaline, and the veteran martial artist might find himself truly fucked in the first two seconds of a real fight. So, it's time to give you some of my broader thoughts about martial arts and street fighting.

I am a big martial arts enthusiast, not just because of the sporting and fitness aspects, but also because I believe they can genuinely add value and strategy to your street fighting. Martial arts strengthened me up in all the right ways – they gave me more speed and accuracy, more dynamic control over my body and footwork, more techniques to use in a scrap. They also helped me to develop a *plan* of how I'm going to fight someone. This might surprise you, because real fights can appear as the ultimate expression of unplanned chaos. But when I can see a fight coming, I always think about my tactics, and quickly.

This process begins as early as possible, my awareness scanning people and the surroundings like a radar. I always size people up when I meet them. I could just be in a coffee shop having a chat, but out the corner of my eye I will be studying the guy stood next to me in the queue, figuring out how capable he is and how I would take him down. For example, I might notice that he has quite skinny legs – I could stamp on his knee. I don't like that guy over there, but he is quite muscular – I could hit him in the throat.

It might sound like the ultimate in paranoia, but I do this all the time, wherever I am, because it's saved me on so many occasions. Every bar I walk into, as soon as I enter I'm assessing all the people around me, working out who is going to be a threatening dick. Then I'll just watch them for a minute or two, seeing if I can pick out any potential weaknesses that I can use against them. I'll also look around the room, the physical space, working out all my fight angles. For example, if I think someone is gonna kick off, I will try to put myself in a position behind him. From this position I can kick out the back of his knee, taking him down to the floor where I can finish him off. If I'm in a room chock full of people, I will always try to position myself in a location where I can take on anybody who might give me some shit, from any angle. I'll also know where all the entrances and exits can be found, and how easy it is to get to them.

I also review my environment for any potential improvised weapons that could be used against me, but also those which I can bring into action myself. For example, I have a habit of standing next to fire extinguishers, because if I have a 'Go!' situation I can pull it off the wall and throw it at someone, or smash him over the head with it. I used to order drinks based on the glasses or bottles they came in. I like those sturdy old pint jugs with a handle – you can really hammer someone with one of those. My mate, John, used to do this as well. We'd go into a bar together and the first drink we would buy would be a bottle of beer. We'd always make sure that we didn't finish completely drain the bottle, so the bar staff would never take it away. This meant that we had an improvised weapon at the ready for the whole evening, ready to twat somebody with it. I probably don't do it as much now, but I'm still hyper aware of everything that's going on around me.

A good weapon can turn a shit fighter into a lethal bastard, so they have to be both expected and respected. Forgot some of the shit you see on TV – you are in serious trouble if someone has a weapon and you don't, especially if it's an edged weapon of any kind. Basically, you have got to use the nastiest techniques possible to stop the guy, ideally by having a weapon of your own. Weapons have been key ingredients of many of the fights I've had, and many of my students have discovered this truth. In fact, some of the wrong 'uns I used to teach in karate would get into proper medieval scraps, with large groups of guys basically attempting to hack or batter each other to bits with whatever they had brought to the fight. One time, they got into a fight with an older, bigger and harder group of lads. My boys knew that they were going to get murdered, so they straight away went for the 'equalisers' – one of them grabbed a claw hammer and the other one a baseball bat. Once they were properly tooled up, they smashed up the other blokes really bad – they remodelled one guy's face with the baseball bat. You do whatever it takes to win. Any different attitude is likely to get you killed.

Details matter in a real fight, everything from your clothing and footwear (try doing some of your martial arts kicks in a pair of heavy boots) to the floor surface and surrounding furniture. Around my late teens, for example, I had a specific 'fight shirt'. My mum had bought this for me one Christmas. It was a collarless 'grandad' shirt, which were quite trendy at the time. At least most of them were trendy, but this one partly slipped through the net. It was an unappealing sludgy brown colour and further murdered fashion by being padded. But there was some logic behind it. My mum's take on it was that because I didn't like wearing a jacket when I was going out, the shirt would keep me warm at night. It was also beer coloured, which meant that it wouldn't show up alcohol stains. But crucially, it also fastened with poppers rather than buttons. This meant that if someone grabbed me by the shirt, the poppers would simply come undone – it would be hard for the other guy to get a grip or any leverage on me. It was also smart enough so that I could get into a club. Everything had a fight logic in my world – it was a proper scrapping shirt. I used to love it.

Returning to the topic of the martial arts, basically they are a great way to keep fit and hone your fighting tools. But as you'll have gathered, that by itself is not going to be enough. The mental game is where it's really at. You could have almost no fight technique to speak off, but if you're an absolute fucking psycho – or you can turn that mindset on at command – then the odds are stacked in your favour.

What happens, and I've seen it hundreds of times, is that the minute a fight becomes real, people panic and basically forget how to fucking move at all, let alone coordinate themselves for the scrap. In a fight, biology matters. When faced with a genuine and immediate threat, your sympathetic nervous system senses fear and goes into overdrive, automatically triggering biological stress reactions, such as the release of adrenaline. We are talking sensory overload here. Your heart rate starts thumping like a machine gun, and your blood vessels dilate. Your breathing quickens and the bronchi in your lungs widen. Your liver increases its conversion of glycogen to glucose. The pupils in your eyes dilate. If you are not used to these sensations, they can feel like shit and root you to the spot. But they are actually serving you well. The increased heart rate and dilated blood vessels, combined with the elevated breathing and expanded bronchi, are working to ensure that your muscles and brain are being fuelled for the fight with oxygenated blood – you actually have your greatest strength, speed and energy at this point. Furthermore, the body stops sending as much blood to any part of the body that doesn't help you survive here and now. It constricts blood flow to your digestive system, for example – you can't afford to waste energy digesting that late-night McDonald's super-size meal, you fat bastard, when it is better used to punch, kick and grapple. Blood also flows away from the skin, which is why people in a scrap often look pale and ill. The production of glucose by the liver gives your muscles and brain an extra kick through a sugar rush. Dilated pupils in your eyes allow more light from your surroundings to rush in, providing you with a sharper visual sense of all the threats around you and facing you.

So all this stress is actually helping you to fulfil the classic 'fight or flight' response. Trouble is, many people in this state just focus on their fear, the consuming terror that their bodily temple is about to get fucking wrecked. What is critical is to get over that initial panic. First, realise that you're not made of glass. In most cases, you're not going to shatter the instant you get twatted. Second, get into the fight straight away – attack genuinely is your best form of defence – ideally before the other guy can land a shot. Nine times out of ten in a street fight, the first person to land a solid shot wins the fight. Even if the opponent doesn't go down straight away, it sets the tune for the whole course of subsequent events. One of my mates used to joke with me that he'd never actually seen me in a street fight, he's just seen me knock lots of people out.

Note that most fights don't start with the first strike, but rather with an exchange of words. The opponent will be squaring up, puffing and pecking, trying to intimidate you with short, shouted phrases. These pre-fight rituals matter. When someone wants to fight you, it's almost like they're trying to convince themselves that you're not really human, to justify the damage they intend to do to you. Most people need to mouth off to build themselves up to the point where they can hit you. Not many people can just unleash their fists without winding themselves up first, like cocking the hammer on a gun. What most people do is get into an argument first and use the momentum of the verbal violence to build up to a physical exchange. How many fights have you actually seen that haven't involved people arguing beforehand? And usually they're just throwing around nonsense words or short, brutal phrases, like, 'You fucking prick!', or 'Come on, fucking come on!' What they are doing is just steeling themselves to fight.

Where I'm different is that I don't argue with people. I might give them a couple of opportunities to calm down and save themselves, but it's often pointless. My dad taught me when I was young that if you were in a pub, and some guy comes up to you and starts mouthing off, if they're not specifically annoyed about something you've done then they're probably just looking for a fight, and nothing's going to steer them away from that. They've most likely had a skinful of drink by that point, so they aren't receptive to reason anyway. If that's the case, don't engage in any argument – take them out straight away with your best monster technique. When someone is giving it the verbals, I always think, 'Why bother?' So as soon as he says to me, 'You're a fucking prick!', BANG! – he's asleep. Seen through this lens, you start to look at your martial arts properly. For example, a nice *kizami-zuki* (straight jab with the front hand) or *gyaku-zuki* (essentially a straight cross-punch with the non-leading hand) might get you a good couple of points when you're competition-sparring, but unless they are backed by real power and aggression they are going to do jack shit on the pavement. The one thing that I do like about KUGB Shotokan karate is the 'One Hit One Kill' ideology – I subscribe to that, although it can be hard to do properly and consistently.

I'll give you an example, a useful early lesson I had. When I was about twelve or thirteen, I got into a fight with a kid I knew. He was a proper fucking bully, actually. He turned his focus onto me before I'd started fighting properly. As a young kid, I'd seen a lot of violence, but I wasn't really toughening up in the way my parents wanted me to. So I faced down some fears and had a fight with this kid. I threw myself into it, my nerves jangling with the rush of energy, sensations that would over time become almost like comfortable slippers, they were so familiar. I'd been doing reasonably well at karate at this stage, so I launched what I thought were some of my best techniques. Looking back, I didn't really have a clue what I was doing, but using a couple of my ambitious kicks I still managed to put him on his arse. He went down in tears, and I stood over him, a young victor. Satisfied that my work was done, I walked away. But as I turned and strutted off, he got to his feet, picked up a nearby loose, house brick, ran up behind me and smashed me over the back of the head with the brick, splitting my scalp open. I had enough reactive presence to turn round and start fighting him again, but then the fight got split up. From that point on, I started to take a lot more notice of fight dynamics, and the strategies for winning.

Never assume a guy is beat. As many of my mates will tell you, for example, I like to get the boot in straight away when a guy is down. I realise that this might seem like an animal move. When I smashed up that guy outside the kebab shop, for example, using his head as a fucking football, my actions might appear to some to be those of a psychopath. But there is a clear logic to it. If you put someone down, you make fucking sure they stay there. If you don't it could be you getting that brick over the back of your head. People are resilient and sly, and in a full-blown street fight the scrap isn't truly over until your opponent's submission is total.

Sometimes people do really ridiculous shit if they aren't used to fighting. There was one time when a guy decided to start on me, and he dropped into a full martial arts stance in front of me, like he was about to unleash his own crouching-wanker style of kung fu. This instantly broadcasted the fact that he'd be fucking useless in a street fight, dropping his guard, pulling his punches and all that shit. I actually pissed myself laughing right in his face. In fact, I couldn't even fight him because I found it so hysterical. Everyone fights different, but you can get a sense when you're stood there whether someone is full of shit or not. Just remember, some people like to stand there, puff their chest out and make themselves look like the big man, but they still might not know how to fight.

A lot of good fight strategy also comes from reading your opponent. Sometimes you get a sense in advance of whether someone is a good fighter or not. His body shape, posture and the way they move can give you clues about whether they can handle themselves or not. A tall, athletic and aggressive-looking fella is naturally likely to cause you more problems than a small, timid and weak bloke, although looks can be deceptive sometimes – never assume a walkover. There is also his demeanour. Is the guy looking confident and cocky or does he have fear written all over his face? If the latter, you have a psychological advantage over him from the start, which you can exploit with terrifying threats and destructive opening attacks.

When you are thinking about your opponents, however, it can be difficult to understand exactly what sort of person you're dealing with. I've got this mate – I definitely can't give you his name – and he likes to do a bit of recreational drugs at the weekend. He's rangy and built like a whippet on an RSPCA poster. At a casual glance, he might give you the impression that he couldn't fight strong winds. But he's no flimsy druggie, he is actually as strong as they fucking come. He looks like an average lad until he takes his shirt off and then you see that he's made of steel and pistons. His muscles have got muscles. He's also quick and, more important, he's totally fearless, bordering on the absolutely bloody mental. He was once faced by a local hard man threatening him with a kitchen knife. His response was not what you'd call orthodox. He wrenched the kitchen knife out of the guy's hand, stabbed *himself* in the stomach, and pulled the blade all the way up to his sternum. Then he said, 'Right, now what they fuck are you going to do to me?' The attacker took one look, shit himself, and legged it. He was right to do so. This is a seriously dangerous sort of guy, because frankly you are going to have to kill him to stop him. He can punch, but he's not particularly well trained. He is strong, but his biggest weapon is that he can go berserk like a Viking in a nunnery. He doesn't give a shit about his own life, so why would he give a shit about yours?

To fight well, you also have to observe a fundamental truth – the only way to win is by hurting the opponent so badly that either pain, injury or loss of consciousness prevents them from continuing. And sometimes, people are built like tanks and just don't seem to get the message, whatever you do. I fought this one guy, a fully grown-ass man, when I was a teenager. I was sat in the bay window of a pub, basically minding my own business. But sometimes, trouble comes looking for me – maybe I've just got one of those faces. Suddenly, the jolly pub atmosphere darkened like fucking Zeus the thunder-god had stepped in for a pint, and this massive bar fight exploded between me and my mates and another group of fellas. Our opponents were actually the local senior men's rugby club – there wasn't a mummy's boy amongst them. I went into action straight away, targeting one guy nearby. He was a big fella, like the by-product of his mum fucking a shire horse. I needed something special to take this guy down. So I leapt off the window into the air, and kicked this big bloke in the face full force. The noise sounded like a pick-axe handle hitting a sandbag, but he just stayed on his feet, recovered from the blow, and came back at me. I unleashed everything I'd got – fists, feet, knees, elbows, fingers, forehead – Christ, I think I considered using my dick as a baton at one point, but he just wouldn't go down. I remember at the time thinking, 'Jesus Christ, I'm in trouble here.'

But sometimes the randomness of fights, plus a bit of improvisation, saves you, and I came out of it alright. He was not down, but he was slightly out on his feet. There were lots of his mates attacking us. I eventually managed to get a grip on things, however, by picking up a barstool (remember what I said about weapons) and smashing the guy in the head with it, hammering hard enough that he started to back off. I also hit a couple of his mates with the stool. By whacking people with the stool, I actually created a sort of safety corridor, like some sort of fucked-up United Nations operation. We used this to escape out of the back door of the pub, then we were over the wall at the back and away. It had been a proper Wild West saloon brawl though – the pub had to close down and rebuild because of all the damage. We actually got quite a bit of local fame for that one. People were talking about it for fucking months. I had survived it, although one of my eyes was an absolute mess.

There have been a few times since when I've fought and thought to myself about my opponent, 'Oh shit, this guy is seriously dangerous.' When I was working as a debt collector (more about that in the next volume), I fought this guy in Manchester. He was fucking terrifying, good with his fists and with that dead look in his eyes that told you he was best mates with violence. He was a really, really good fighter, and in fairness he nearly beat the fuck out of me. Here's how it played out.

It was meant to be a straightforward home-by-dinner-time debt collection job. I'd been told in advance that the other guy was a 'little bit handy, but nothing special'. They lied fucking outrageously – he was a first-class street fighter, known far and wide for being a hard nut. It turns out that as well as being a brickie by trade, he'd also won several championships as an amateur boxer and had served four years in prison for assault. I was trying to get money out of someone who employed him and he took exception to it, and to me.

What really annoyed me afterwards was that when it came to the fight, he totally got the drop on me. Accompanied by a mate, I went round to collect the money from one of those grim estates where the tarmac is always sticky with blood. We walked in like a couple of right Wombles, straight into a viper's den of hardmen and local crooks, a real melting pot of nasty arseholes. I didn't like doing stuff like this, but I was absolutely skint at the time. Anyway, we headed to the designated premises and instantly everything went tits up. My mate wasn't doing the proper reconnaissance, and this fighter guy came at me from a blind spot and twatted me on the side of the face. His punch was like being hit by a 12-gauge shotgun blast. Luckily, I managed to stay on my feet, because if I'd gone to the ground he would've started converting my head into a pizza with his boots. But I was now proper woozy, and there were a barrage of punches coming in at me hard and fast. So I played hedgehog – I wrapped my head in my hands, kept moving and tried to recover myself to get back into the fight. I managed to start sending out my own punches into this guy's body and face, giving him a bit of his own damage to deal with. But then there was a weird natural break in the fight and we managed to negotiate a bit, resolving things without taking it through to final victory or defeat.

To be frank, I was lucky. You have to be honest about fighting – if that one had continued, I'm not sure it would've ended in my favour. Even if he hadn't caught me with the initial blow, I still think it would have been a close-run thing. I was in survival mode. Usually I try to plan a fight, but this time there was no planning and I was simply struggling to stay the right side of consciousness.

Nobody is invincible, but then again it depends on whether you care or not. I've spent quite a long time being largely indifferent whether I live or not in a fight, and that makes a hell of a difference. Ultimately I'm only meat, blood, bone and some liquid (spoiler: so are you), so I'm not sure I give much of a fuck.

There are lots of martial artists out there who have never been in a real fight. The uncertainty about how they would do in a street battle really preys on their minds. My advice? First, you have to test yourself before you even get into a street fight. What a lot of people don't realise is that you can partially replicate the natural adrenaline rush of a fight in different situations. This can be anything that scares you. For example, I'm not particularly fond of heights, but when I was working as a roofer I used to walk across steel beams that were 200 feet up in the air. It gave me arse-puckering terror, but I had to get used to the anxiety by facing it – there was no other way. So, accustom yourself to doing things that scare you or even just make you feel uncomfortable, whatever they might be. Never back away from them.

Then there's the matter of how you train in the martial arts. It's sometimes hard for me to give advice here, because I've been fighting practically my whole life, so for me that experience is normal. Sometimes I don't even get the adrenaline rush anymore, it's just business as usual. But the training rule is: Train as hard as you fight. If you spar with realism and danger, taking hard hits and giving them back, you'll start to build up the fight mentality, plus you'll get used to the adrenaline sensations and you'll be less likely to be paralysed by them in a real fight. If you get the right instructor, even very traditional karate will seriously toughen you up. The trouble is that there are a lot of dickhead instructors out there, ones who don't really know what they are doing. A good, solid instructor will implement a programme of hard sparring, where you actually experience fear inside the *dojo*. This will hone your fight skills enormously.

In terms of what type of martial art you should do, I recommend that you have a core discipline in which you really become an expert, but mix it up with some other disciplines to round off your bag of techniques. I've done Wado Ryu karate, Kyokushinkai karate, freestyle kickboxing, Shotokan karate, Muay Thai, boxing, wrestling, and picked up loads of other stuff. I also happened on some good instructors who really focused on the *kumite*; at the end of every session we put on all the headgear and pads and would beat the shit out of each other. At the Muay Thai club, it was all full-contact as well. To summarise for someone who is training in the martial arts and who has never had a fight: find good instructors who understand *kumite* and do lots of heavy sparring, plus, mix your main discipline up by going to different clubs and training in different martial arts and combat sports.

I'm going to stick my neck out here though and say that there's too much hype around Brazilian Jujitsu (BJJ) at the moment. Grappling has got its uses, don't get me wrong, grappling is great. It's not so good, however, when you're fighting someone with multiple mates in a real fight situation. They'll quite happily let you go to the floor, because there they will kick the fuck out of you. I find that nowadays a lot of door staff are trained in jujitsu. A bouncer I once beat up was one of them, but BJJ didn't do him much good when I was smashing him in the side of the face with my fists and elbows.

Let me give you an analogy to clarify the point. Within the British armed forces, we've got the Army, Navy and Air Force. Each service of the armed forces works in support of the others, but with an entirely different set of tactics and tools. For example, the Air Force will help the Army by bombing the crap out of enemy positions in front of the advance on the ground. But the Air Force cannot take and hold enemy cities – you need good old infantry for that. But neither the Air Force nor the Army can control the seas, that's the Navy's job. In a similar way, your fight techniques need to cover all the bases – close range, medium range and long range. When you're fighting at close range, grappling certainly comes into play, but there's other devastating stuff as well, like knees and elbows. Fuck I've even bitten people in street fights. And before you get to the close fighting, try to finish the scrap with long-range or medium-range techniques like kicks and punches. Punches themselves can work from long to close range, starting with stretched-out long jabs, transitioning through shorter, more powerful crosses and wide-swinging hooks, and closing in, to short-range hooks and uppercuts. The point is, you need to be well rounded. So, grappling is great, but it's not enough on its own. If you are training in jujitsu or something like that, you want to be doing something like boxing as well. A lot of people don't bother with boxing anymore. But you can't beat a proper boxing session, when you are in close, using your hands, taking constant shots to the face and body. As a form of combat training, I'd argue that it's superior to many other types.

While I'm having a rant, I've also got a bit of a problem with Mixed Martial Arts (MMA). I was watching some a while ago, and the commentators were singing the praises of this professional, saying that he was a seasoned veteran because he had been training for four years. In what fucking sense is he a veteran in anything? He might only have had five or six proper professional fights in his career. Don't get me wrong, these guys are super fit and they do put the work in, but there are a lot of them (with the exception of some of the really top guys) who have done a little bit of lots of things and rolled it all together without mastering anything in particular. I've been doing karate now for the best part of forty years, and I've risen high up its ranks, yet although many people do regard me as an expert, I don't regard myself as a master. People who have been training for five years are, to me, people who are just starting out. MMA is certainly entertaining to watch, but it's now become its own form of martial art and that's not what it was intended to be. It's Mixed Martial Arts – people who do it are reasonable at a few different things, but in my opinion they're not learning enough of a core skill.

There's also a massive difference between real violence and MMA violence, as brutal as the fight cage can seem. We still have to recognise that MMA is sport fighting. In street violence, any technique, any weapon, any strategy is on the table. Even in the hard knocks of the MMA cage, no one is going to drive a pencil into your eyeball or attempt to spill your brains with a house brick. There is also no tap-out or responsible referee waiting to stop the fight the moment a person looks like he is getting seriously hurt.

Compare an MMA cage fight with one real-world street fight of mine: This was all happening outside a club where I was working in an unofficial capacity. A problem I've always had is that I keep getting shoehorned into security roles, even when I'm meant to be doing something else. At this particular club I'd been employed as a fucking glass collector, not an on-call hitman. Anyway, I ended up throwing a guy out of the club and after that it all went wrong. It wasn't particularly intense at first, we just exchanged a few insults and then began trading hands. But while I was slogging it out with this guy, his sneaky fucking mate came up behind me and literally wrapped his arms around me in a crushing bear hug. He picked me up off the ground. So I'm now stuck like a twat, feet off the floor and my arms pinioned to the side of my body. I'm thrashing my head backwards to try to reverse head-butt him to get him off me. While I'm doing this, the original guy I was fighting looks really happy about the way things are panning out, and now starts smashing me in the face of his fists. By wriggling like a salmon on a riverbank, I managed to push the bear-hug guy back up against a wall. But I just couldn't get him off me and I was having no success in trying to nut him with the back of my skull.

Then came the moment of transition. I'm not sure how it happened, but we all managed to get squashed in by the side of some wheelie bins. The guy who was hitting me at this point suddenly lost balance and stumbled forward, crashing into me. His face was just inches from mine, so I took the opportunity and sank my teeth into his face. I got my fangs clamped down deep into his cheek and I was ragging the flesh. I was literally gnawing on his face like Hannibal Lecter having Sunday lunch. People underestimate teeth as a weapon. The power you can exert through your jaw is phenomenal and the pain inflicted is stratospheric. The guy holding me now let go just through sheer shock at what I was doing. Silly fuck – this allowed me to break away and turn the tables in my favour. I proceeded to beat the living shit out of both of them. The guy who I had bitten was screaming and holding his ruined face, so while he was preoccupied I kicked him hard in the bollocks. He went down and out. I turned on the other guy, grabbed him by one ear, and drove his head about five or six times into the wall behind him, until he gave up the fight. My girlfriend at the time was really pissed off at me when I returned home with a cut-up face – I'd only nipped out for a quiet pint.

Compare this fight to a risk-free semi-contact martial arts competition or the limited violence of the MMA cage, and hopefully you'll see that training for street fighting requires a whole different mentality. But now, as we return to the narrative of my life, it was a mentality I would need by the ton.

CHAPTER 5 DARK WORLD

I can hear you thinking, 'Conrad, given that you were spending all your time being a dodgy bastard, how did you find time for romance?' (Actually, I can't hear anything except a deafening fucking silence.) As far as my romantic life was concerned around this time, I didn't really have girlfriends, at least not proper ones in the conventional sense. I certainly had girls who I used to fuck every now and again. In fact, I was actually doing quite well shagging the karate students up at the university. Talk about batting above your average. The girls in college were at the absolute top of their physical game, mostly between eighteen and twenty-one years old and unleashed from the inhibitory gaze of their mum and dad for the first time. So why they paired up with me, a sixteen-year-old youth, is worth a pause for thought.

Certainly, there are all types of ladies in the world, and standards are massively variable, but I do like to think that I was mature for my age – many of the people around me just didn't have a clue I was still of school age. Certainly, I was a big lad, but in all honesty, I think that many of the posh university girls simply liked a bit of rough. I exuded what youngsters today refer to as 'big dick energy'. I was regarded as something of a karate hardman, so the girls were attracted to the rebel, the classic 'bad boy'. Also, as much as I was fighting all the time, I was pretty good company to people who I liked.

I can be generous, I think, with my time, money and attention, so I used to get on with people, girls included.

Weirdly, I suddenly became aware that girls might be attracted to me, when I broke my pelvis in the garage inspection-pit fall. All of a sudden, there were loads of attractive girls coming to visit me in hospital. Impressively, I actually had sex in the hospital while I was physically on traction – amidst all the straps and pulleys the scene looked like some deviant German dungeon porn film, but it did me the power of good. Later, I remember coming out of hospital and pondering, 'Hold on, I think that one of those girls really fancies me.' The girl in question was two years older than me, at an age when subtle age differences seem to count. But I'm a defiant sod, and thought 'Fuck it, I'm just going to try it on with her.' And I did and it was right, and it worked. I had my first proper girlfriend.

That was a bit of a turning point for me. I realised that when it came to the opposite sex, it didn't really matter too much what you look like. I wasn't unattractive, but nor was I in any way a high-status Brad Pitt. Let's say I was a five on the classic attractiveness scale. I was average looking. But I realised that if you don't ask you don't get. I also wised up to the fact that if you have a ton of confidence, a friendly manner, a decent athletic body and a bit of notoriety, you could jack yourself up from a five to a fucking eight or nine.

I suddenly acquired an adrenaline shot of swagger. If the Queen of Spain and an Austrian super-model had been in the same room, I would have had a crack at arranging a threesome. Whereas a lot of my mates were getting other guys to go and tell a girl that they liked her, I would just walk straight up, doing the whole strong eye-contact thing, and say, 'I like you, what do you reckon?' And while I occasionally crashed and burned, many, many times it just fucking worked. The direct approach, especially to teenage girls (when I was a teenager of course), really paid off because other guys just didn't do that. You separated yourself from the herd.

My new-found confidence with females, however, did create complications, especially up at the university club where I was teaching. I ended up copping off with this girl called Belinda. I was sixteen and she was seeing my older mate, Jack, at the time. Not for long fucking long.

It all happened after a karate competition in Keele. The whole team was piled up at the bar after the competition, swapping fight stories and drifting inevitably into alcoholic flirtation. Belinda was proper into me, sitting close and saying how impressed she was with my performance during the fights. I can remember just leaning in and kissing her, bold as brass. We had a bit of a snog, and when we broke away, she said, 'Well that was unexpected.'

I replied, 'Fuck off, I've been lining up for that all day.' So we ended up having quite a fun, flirtatious evening. Of course, like an episode of fucking *Love Island*, the truth soon came out. Jack went fucking mental. He straight away told her that I was only sixteen, which based on her wide-eyed shock obviously came as unwelcome news. It also really scuppered my chances of actually getting a shag. When she found out that she was about to cop off with someone who intermittently wore school uniform, she disappeared pretty rapidly.

But while Belinda slipped the net, the university provided me with lots of other opportunities which took me all the way into port. As dodgy as it sounds today, during Freshers' Week me and one of the other instructors would basically look at all the new recruits and divide up who would get first dibs when it came to shagging specific girls. The problem was that I started to get a bit of a reputation around the university and town as a shagger as well as a nutter, which tended to scare off some of the nice girls (not all of them though). But other girls, truth be told, are drawn exactly to that type, so I was kept busy. Around this time, I also ended up managing a local sports shop in the town centre, as well as running the karate club. Add the fact that I wasn't paying any rent, I actually had a bit of money on me, which can also oil the wheels of romance. Most of my other mates were still at school, university or were unemployed, so they were skint, pushing the boat out by offering a girl a bag of chips and a battered sausage. I realised that I could pretty much do whatever I wanted, so I did.

My success with girls could, however, could produce some absolutely laughable situations. One of them occurred previously, when I was acting as a referee at a karate competition. At the start of the female *kumite*, all the referees were called together for a briefing and we were asked to declare any personal connections to the females about to fight. I sheepishly raised my hand and informed the others that I'd actually slept with all of them. I bet that's not a problem faced by the umpires at Wimbledon!

Now, this all might sound like life's a riot. But at the same time I was suffering some pretty serious mental health issues, so all the fun played out under low, black rainclouds in my mind. As mentioned previously, I'm autistic, but this wasn't diagnosed until my late thirties, so I struggled on with this condition without anybody, including myself, understanding what was going on inside me. School had been an embarrassing disaster – I couldn't even spell my own name properly until I was about twelve or thirteen. I was pretty good at maths, but I couldn't handle any written work. So I was basically left to my own devices in school and largely ignored. Not only did I not understand schoolwork, I didn't really want to do it anyway. When I moved to *T*—, however, everything got even worse because most of the lessons were conducted in Welsh, and I couldn't speak a word. So I was an undiagnosed autistic lad from a violent background, who could barely read or write in English, who suddenly found himself in a Welsh-speaking school.

A mind under pressure, struggling to survive, develops some odd coping mechanisms. I remember having a bit of obsessive compulsive disorder (OCD) in school, extending into my late teens and early adulthood. There were certain rituals I just had to perform if I was to get to sleep at night, such as repeating specific rhymes from beginning to end. As another example, I had a little coin bag that I used to take with me to competitions – I absolutely had to have it with me to ensure I went into the fight with confidence. I also had to tie my shoes up in a certain way.

Regular life doesn't always bend itself to your needs, and if I couldn't do things my way then I'd have a problem. And I don't mean a bit of minor anxiety or blowing into a paper bag – someone was going to get smashed in the face. To be honest, I think my autism was the key reason why I fought so much when I was growing up. I also struggled to cope in sensory overload environments, such as school discos – I've since found out that that is one of the key symptoms of autism.

There are also some real nightmare corners of my childhood, ones that have left some nasty ghosts at the end of dark corridors. Let's just say that I was 'interfered' with when I was small, and it made me quite dark in personality. It might sound weird, but I used to struggle mentally if I felt happy, like my immune system was fighting the invasion of a foreign body. Even to this day, if I sense that I'm becoming genuinely happy, I'll start to kick and scream against it, hunting out the antidote that will return me to a more familiar depression and anger.

Let me show you how it could express itself. Back in the day, I'd gone out with my mates to a club. It was panning out to be a good evening. I felt on top of my flirting game and I got talking to one particular girl, a proper raise-the-dead stunner, on the way in. I remember that she had a graceful tattoo on her back, the lines of ink curling around the delicate muscles, framed by a slender waist atop undulating dancer's hips. At the time, tattoos we're quite rare on girls – people weren't as inked up as they are now. But I remember finding this tattoo the sexiest thing ever, so the I opened the taps on every seduction technique in the book. I was soon making progress, as well. I found myself locked in a passionate kiss with the girl, my state of arousal hitting DEFCON 1 and about go full nuclear.

I suddenly became conscious that it was turning out to be the best evening ever. I'm out with my mates. Everyone's laughing and dicking about. I've got good money in my pocket. I've had a few beers. Capping it all off, I'm with this gorgeous girl – she chose *me*. And all this was too much – here was the trigger. Within about five minutes of that clear-eyed moment of happiness, I was violently brawling with a group of farmers. Instead of fun and beauty, there's blood, ugliness, crying girls, pain and disorder. What used to happen was that in social situations I would reach a point or place where I just didn't know how to act, so I would revert back to what I was good at, which was fighting. If somebody so much as bumped into me in this state of mind, that was it – the fists were up and I was gone, into the fight zone. If someone looked at me wrong, I socked them. The truth is, even today I almost find violence a comforting thing. I don't fight because I'm angry, I fight because it makes me feel better. It restores the situation to an honest interaction. I know how fucked-up this sounds, and today I can recognise the symptoms coming on and take avoidance measures. But the trigger is always there, waiting to be pulled.

To understand more deeply where I'm coming from, you've also got to appreciate my worldview, which as you might expect isn't exactly covered with glitter and baubles. Generally, people are shit. There are very, very few people who I really trust. In my experience, people almost inevitably screw you over most of the time, or at least eventually. I personally know hundreds of people, but the number of people I chat to regularly and closely you can count on the fingers of one hand.

I'm quite good at getting along to people, hence I've been pretty successful in business over my time. But I will still keep most humans at arm's length. I almost always find that interactions with people are very false. My wife Chloe, by contrast, is super-gregarious and gets on with almost everybody in the world – she's really outgoing (more about her later). Furthermore, when people let her down, it doesn't really bother her – she's very forgiving and accepts people's failings. With me it's different. I form true friendships with very few people, and if any of those people do let me down, it really stings.

I'll give you an example from a bit later in my life narrative.

As you'll find out in the next volume, I had a very successful security business for a time. Cash was just pouring in through a high-pressure hose, and life was approaching idyllic. At the time, we lived in this very affluent village, truly at the heart of the leafy, prosperous community. We were integrated into a group of about ten families and we all became very close, with lots of socialising under sunny skies. Every time someone had a birthday, we would all descend on their house for a party. We used to go away camping for the weekends as an enormous pack. Every Saturday someone would be having a barbecue or a house party or something. There must've been about forty kids at some of these events, all playing happily with one another as the adults got gently sozzled together. I know that we used to get a bit of flak around the village because we partied hard, but it was all good-natured and friendly. There was never any trouble. It was comfortable, lovely, relaxing. It had that slightly timeless feel of a place where you just belong.

To be honest, I initially hated doing all the convivial shit, for reasons I've just explored. But after a year of open-door mingling, I started to get really close to a few of them. I used to talk with them a lot more, opening up about myself and my life in a way I hadn't previously. For one guy's fortieth birthday party, I supplied all the bouncy castles, the bar, all the security, all for no charge. I wasn't drinking at the time, so I would always be offering myself up as the designated driver, running people home at the end of the night and making sure that they home got safe through their front doors. I didn't care, I just enjoyed the night out.

But life had other plans. The business went tits up and me and the wife lost our house. Then we lost everything else. Socially, it was like we had stepped into an elevator and someone cut the cable, leaving us to plunge to the bottom while everyone else remained at the top, letting us fall. All of a sudden, most of them didn't want to talk to us anymore. They just switched off. Chloe, with all her loveliness, managed to stay polite when we bumped into them in supermarkets, but I would be instantly confrontational – 'Fuck you! You're not my friend! I don't even need anything from you, I just need you to be a mate. You won't speak to me because I've lost everything, so go fuck yourself.' I was totally unforgiving.

Before this all happened, I'd had one of the nicest houses in the village and lots of people who I thought were my mates. I had high-end cars, celebrity mates and ran society parties. Sure, some used to joke that they thought I was secretly in the mafia, but actually people wanted to know about all that shit, they would get a kick out of it. But as soon as we had nothing, they all vanished. When I turned up at the school to drop the kids off – the same kids who had up until recently been playing with theirs – half the fuckers wouldn't even look me in the eye.

We were eventually placed into a hotel while we tried to get housing, but this hotel was fifteen fucking miles away from where we took the kids to school. I was absolutely skint and the school wouldn't provide transport for the kids. They basically said we would have to change the kids' school, which we weren't going to do because the accommodation was purely temporary. The kids had already experienced enough disruption without forcing them to go into another school, and likely a shit one full of the usual infant predators from rough areas. So every morning I would get a taxi from the hotel to the school, dropping the kids off. But because I had almost no money, I would then walk the fifteen miles back. And this went on for three months. Now a lot of these cunts knew what was going on. Most of them worked in L— where they headed after dropping the kids off, so they could've taken me at least ten miles closer to the hotel, or God forbid actually run me straight to it. In those three months, I think that in total there were only four occasions when people actually gave me a lift to the hotel. Some of them even drove past me while I was walking on the road in the pissing rain.

Now you might be thinking that there's more to it than this. Maybe I'm not telling you everything, and I'd done something deeper to cause the blanket rejection. But what happened next completes the picture: If life gives me a kicking, I won't stay down for long. Before you know it, I clawed my way back on to my feet. Money and work started to come in again, including some celebrity stuff. We managed to pull together enough to buy a nice little bungalow in the village, with three acres of land, all within a year of my being on my arse. Then, hey fucking presto, suddenly all the old gang start appearing again, knocking on my door, flashing their big smiles and party invites. I was less than welcoming, asking them 'What the fuck do you want?' before closing the door in their faces.

I might be from the wrong side of the tracks, but if one of my mates have been in similar trouble, I would be picking them up from the hotel every morning. I wouldn't have asked them for anything, I'd just want to do what I could to get them back on their feet. It's called fucking loyalty. When things were at their worst, it would have made a big difference just for someone to have been friendly. I once jokingly said to my wife that one day I was going to build a fence around the entire village and burn the fucking place down. (If there are any police reading this, don't get your helmet wobbling – I am fucking joking.)

The trouble is, I just can't help holding a grudge. I've got a highly developed sense of justice, even if I know that it's misplaced on occasions. If someone does something to me, I have to do something back – I can't just leave it and take in the bigger picture. My sense of retribution can survive decades. I was in a park in the north of England a few years ago and I spotted this other guy. Something about him triggered a recognition, and an age-old grudge. It was a kid, now all grown up, who

I'd been in primary school with, and back then he'd been a right cunt to me. So, forgetting the fact that people are capable of evolving and changing, I went over and told him to go fuck himself. He was shocked, I have to say, not least because he could barely remember me. The confrontation developed into a proper argument, and I then made it clear to him that if he didn't back off, I would drop him. He saw sense and went off in a strop. My grudge had crossed thirty years of time. I was totally prepared to fight him because he had pissed me off in primary school. My wife just looked at me and said, 'I really, really think you need to talk to someone about this.' I know that he walked away without having a fucking clue, to this day, why I intended to smash him.

I recognise that it would be easier on me if I looked at things the way that other people do. But bear with me, there is some logic in here. Take keyboard warriors, for example. There are loads of people who sit in front of a computer and slag off everybody else in the world. They do this because they are safe and they can get away with it. If fewer of those sort of people were safe, *physically*, I reckon we'd have fewer arseholes in the world. There's this one guy I know who is a right weedy little cunt, but online he's the gob-shite heavyweight champion of the world, spouting out all sorts of aggressive shit. He has horrible opinions about people, and he's rude to them all the time. But I know that if the first time he was vile to someone he got his teeth pushed in by a fist, he wouldn't be rude to anyone else subsequently. He would have

106

been rewired to be more cautious. Far too many people now can get away with being horrible because there are no real consequences. I believe that if people knew that there would be physical consequences for their behaviour, in general they would be a lot nicer. Sure, there'll be a lot more violence in the beginning, but then it would all even out. If you think that this just sounds like a recipe for anarchy, just look at see how the tolerant approach is working out for society.

I also think that a lot of gentle society just doesn't have a fucking clue how rough the world is out there. They *think* they know because they read the unpleasant stories in the *Guardian*, but they don't feel or see the reality for themselves. They don't know the fear, the dirtiness human character can attain. I can give you a recent example. There was a guy outside one of my shops a few weeks ago. Although the shop is positioned right in the centre of an apparently pleasant tourist town, trouble often flows past the doors, especially at night. This fella, he had half of his head split open – he looked like he'd been bottled. One of my guys, Dave, spotted this and decided to do the right thing, and went out to help him. I was suspicious. Sometimes helping out certain people means that you get sucked into their vortex of shit, and they don't even thank you for it. Plus, there were lots of other people around to cause problems. 'Nah, just fucking leave it,' I said, but Dave went out anyway. He can handle himself, so I wasn't too worried.

By the time he crosses the street, the guy's lying on the floor, there's blood everywhere and he's trying to keep his head shut with his fingers. There are lots of people around him, some making empty offers of help, but most just wanting to have a story to tell later. Dave says to him, 'Do you want me to call you an ambulance?'

One of the guy's mates is there, and he says, 'Yeah, yeah, call an ambulance.' Dave does so, and while they wait, he asks the injured fella what happened.

He replies, 'I was sucking this guy's dick out on the street and I suddenly fell backwards and smashed my head on the wall.'

To be honest, it's not the answer Dave was expecting, and he was completely thrown by it, and spluttered out, 'You were doing fucking what?!' He had scarcely finished the sentence before loads of people around him whipped out their camera phones and started filming him, suddenly accusing him of being homophobic. Bear in mind that at this moment he's the only one who's actually trying to help and call an ambulance, and that he was shocked because someone was gobbling off another bloke in broad daylight with lots of families milling about.

In my view, this pretty much sums up our society. He's going to help a guy, he was a little bit thrown by what he heard, then, all of a sudden, he's the bad guy. When I got wind of this, I decided I was going to go over there, take everybody's phones and beat the fuck out of them all. Wiser heads prevailed and I was persuaded not to. My point is that there was no consequence for being a wanker. All these lads, mates of the guy on the floor, were outside accusing us of being homophobic, not realising that pretty much all our staff are either gay or bisexual. We are the least homophobic shop in the town.

To bring my rant to a conclusion in the simplest terms, I've had a lot of really bad stuff happen to me over my life and a lot of supposedly good friends who turned out to be absolute shits. On the whole, with a few exceptions as rare as a dick in a nunnery, people are bad.

CHAPTER 6 ON THE JOB

Time to lighten the mood a bit. Returning to my late teens, one of those periodic changes of direction came about. When I was eighteen and no longer in education, I worked for a time as a butcher in a supermarket, spending my whole day preparing chops and joints, coming home smelling of meat and blood. Then I became the manager of a local sports shop. This job was okay, as I was well into fitness, but I was also getting into a lot of trouble. Predictably, I got restless with this life and I moved back to Cardiff shortly after,

Throughout my school years, Cardiff had pulled me back on a regular basis. From the age of about fourteen or fifteen, I was spending most of my summers down in Cardiff. How it used to work was that if my brothers needed labourers on the building site, I'd simply stop going to school for a while and head down there to work, lying about my age to the authorities. However, I moved from A— back to Cardiff, completely, when I was about eighteen. So my brother rang and asked me, 'Why don't you come and do some building work for me?' And so began my career in the building trade, which was fucking hilarious. The first day on the job set the scene – instead of going to work we just all bunked off and went bowling instead. Compounding the fun, I still got paid for it. This was just the beginning of a wild ride in the construction business.

Much of the building industry is dodgy to the core. My brother's company did a lot of work for a crooked building surveyor, who in turn handled a lot of big-money contracts for the local city council. There was a major rejuvenation project underway in Riverside, which, let's say, was one of the more colourful parts of the city. It was a weird place. It was quite downtrodden, but at the same time the homes were fucking great, these really lovely old town houses. But they were worth fuck-all and had families of about fifty in them. In response, the council basically threw around loads of money trying to do these houses up until they were fit for habitation. In their wisdom, they gave the contract to my brother, which in retrospect was a decision as fucking stupid as sending unattended kids to the moon.

The first thing you should know about my brother is that he didn't really have a clue what he was doing. This applied both to running a business and to the practical skills of building. Half the time we used to make stuff up, inventing some of the world's worst building techniques and charging a fuck-off price for them. When we were particularly clueless, we'd take a break from internet porn to consult Google or YouTube about building techniques. Sometimes we ended up going to other building sites and asking legit builders what the hell were doing, and could they show us how to do it. My brother was actually a roofer, and to be fair he was pretty good at that. Everything else was a rocky voyage on the sea of incompetence.

Like attracts like, which probably goes a long way to explaining how my brother got in with this dodgy building surveyor. Being equally bent meant they could rely on each other to shaft the system. (Just an interesting aside – the surveyor, whose name I won't mention, spent loads of money giving his son a private education. The investment was truly money down the fucking toilet – because eventually that lad went into being a cameraman on porn films, which we just thought was the funniest thing ever.) Then there was this other guy, who was a super-rich pilot. He was actually funding the whole thing. What they were making out of it, I don't know, but I do know that the money was basically being delivered by the bale. We were doing alright, but they were doing *really* well.

This is how it worked: The main building contract came in, and after that had been completed there were the 'snagging' lists to look after. Say, for example, the builders had to rebuild a house. Once the house was completed and the main contractor had moved on, an inspector would come in and evaluate the property for outstanding issues, such as a problem with plastering or a doorframe that wasn't fitted properly. The snagging list basically contained things that were missed by the original builders. So they employed my brother's company to go round and handle the snagging list – we fixed all the fuck-ups, basically. What this meant in practical terms was that we had snagging list for two to three hundred houses, pages of minor jobs that could keep us going forever. Remember also that these were the days when mobile phones weren't common at all, so we got paid to go around knocking on doors. If the occupants were home and they were happy to let us in, we would go in and do the work. If they weren't happy, or they weren't at home, we'd simply move onto the next one. It was pretty much a licence do whatever we fucking wanted.

We weren't paid by the job, but instead we were on a day rate. There were five of us and each of us was getting paid a hundred quid a day, which doesn't sound much now, but back then it was pretty decent coin. Perhaps partly realising that we were a bunch of cowboys, the council gave us a van with a tracker in it, to make sure that we were where we were supposed to be. It didn't take us long to get this one cracked. What we would do was get someone to travel to the destination, park up the van for five minutes, and then just drive up and down the road. While one person was doing this, the dodgy surveyor set us up with loads of jobs on the side. So we were all skimming off the council contract, while at the same time doing lots of private work – the money was absolutely rolling in. Some days we would even head into work and think, 'Fuck it!', park the van up, put a bit of sealant around some guy's window (which took all of five minutes) and then just go to the pub.

We could take dicking about and wasting time to whole new levels of outrageous front. A glacier could carve out a fucking valley in the Alps quicker than it took

113

us to complete a day's work. One day in 1998, for example, Emperor Akihito of Japan came over to visit Cardiff Castle. We were supposed to be working, as always, but instead we were down at the castle. A major national newspaper didn't want the visit to take place because of Japanese wartime atrocities, so they went the extra mile to be offensive and had produced these cut-out-and-wear Japanese masks that were, looking back, really racially insulting. So we went and joined the anti-Japanese protest crowd, all kitted out in these masks and totally pissed up. We had absolutely nothing against the emperor, in fact most of us wouldn't have been able to pick him out from a police line-up. We were just fucking bored.

But in many ways, at least joining a protest had a socially responsible element to it. Other stuff we did really closed the gates of heaven. For example… if one of these residents was actually stupid enough to let us in to do the work, we would always find an excuse to go up on the roof of these long rows of terraced houses. Once we were up there, we'd run down to the other end of the terrace with a roofing axe and make holes in the lead work or smash lots of tiles. Then we'd come down, faces a picture of innocence, and leave the area… until it was raining. As soon as there was a downpour, we'd be back on the street driving up and down, knocking on the doors and asking if they had any leaks. Of course they did, because we'd basically fucking ruined their roofs. They would go up into the attics and find water pissing

114

in, so they would book us for the job. Then we charge them about ninety quid a tile to fix it. We knew the houses that were fucked because we'd fucked them up. Jesus.

The other thing that we would sometimes do is go up onto people's roofs and nick all their lead flashing and guttering, throw it into next door's garden, then take it away. We'd then go and sell the lead for scrap and at the same time charge the household for replacing the lead that we had nicked in the first place. Or we would go and chop holes in the guttering and tell them that their guttering was fucked and needed replacing. Then we'd just fill the holes with sealant so that the guttering would stop leaking and we charge them for reapplying lead to the whole roof, whereas in reality we'd just filled the holes with a bit of sealant.

I know, I know… you are starting to hate us. I can't say anything in defence, except that this culture of shafting people was virtually standard in much of the construction industry at that time. We just took it to the next level.

What fucked all this up for us was that my brother got caught for stealing. Also, I got accused of doing something which, for once, I actually fucking didn't do. I was accused of nicking some guy's Rayban glasses. He came out onto the street shouting at us in the van, saying that I had nicked his glasses from his house. In my wisdom, I thought the right thing to do in response was to get out of the van, deny his accusations, then headbutt

115

him in the face after he gave me a shove. Believe it or not, that wasn't the best option. All of a sudden, all the houses emptied of people and in an instant there were fucking thousands of this guy's mates surrounding us. I only found out afterwards that he was a well-known local drug dealer.

The situation did get a bit hairy. To make matters worse, this guy's brother came out armed with a fucking crossbow and made preparations to shoot me with it. He pointed it at me, and the fact that I was about to be skewered by a 20-inch bolt prompted my brother and another of our gang, Nickie, to get out of the van to sort him out. Nickie was absolutely wired for a fight – he was the type of guy who dropped speed for breakfast.

My brother said to crossbow man, 'You've got one arrow and there are three of us. So the minute you fire that, the other two will fucking kill you.' Luckily this urban Rambo bottled it, but I actually thought I was going to die that day. We did get reported for that incident, but the council knew the crossbow guy was a drug dealer, so they didn't give a fuck. I actually hadn't stolen anything, although to be fair it's quite likely that my brother did. The thing is that we were answering to the surveyor, who under his veneer of respectability was covering our arses while we were getting up to all sorts. Occasionally the council would ask us what we had actually done that week, but we'd cook up all sorts of excuses: 'We were doing a roofing job, but then the owner went mental and threw us all out.' or, 'We had to leave because they had an aggressive dog.' – that sort of thing. We could always blag it.

Now all this went on for two-and-a-half years. We made an absolute fortune. Don't get me wrong, some days we would work really hard and totally legitimately. But what would happen is suddenly we'd get a private job. Then we would go into overdrive. We could strip and re-tile an entire roof in just one day between the four of us (believe me, this is fucking intergalactic speed) and we had to do it that fast so the council didn't get wind of where we were. I was also driving the van, which I shouldn't have been doing because I didn't have a driving licence.

The lack of driving licence is worth exploring a bit more. It was yet another example of the way I didn't exactly have a normal childhood. When I was about fifteen, my dad had an accident. We are not talking a nasty gash to the arm here – he was crushed by a JCB digger. He had been working on a forestry project and a JCB got caught in a landslide. Several tons of industrial vehicle went free-sliding down an embankment. As it came to a stop the solid-steel bucket turned and crushed my dad's leg into the ground. I think he had about a hundred and fifty breaks in his leg. Unsurprisingly, he was in hospital for absolute ages – a good eighteen months. The unexpected upshot of this was that I had to learn to drive.

My mum simply didn't like driving through the winding country lanes, especially at night, so the natural solution was to let her fifteen-year-old son take the wheel. I got the hang of it pretty quickly – me and my mates had been dicking about with vehicles for years. So I used to drive from *T*— to *A*— all the time in my dad's car. I'd drive my mum to the hospital, drop her off, go training then go out on the piss afterwards. Occasionally I would maximise the fucking insanity by driving home pissed, all at the age of fifteen.

My new-found freedom behind the wheel became normal, and I find normality really fucking dull. So then me and my mate Danny used to try to push the boundaries, pretending we were rally drivers and all that. One epic thing we'd do is swap drivers while we were driving. One of us would go from the passenger seat across, while the driver, whoever that was, would go from the driver's seat out the side window, climb across the roof rack, and come back in through the passenger window. We got really good at doing this at about 60mph. We used to do stuff like this all the time. Or four of us would all switch places within the car. It looked like a bunch of fucking monkeys looting a family car at a safari park. We were pure-bred idiots. We nearly killed Danny, because while he was on the roof one time I think we hit a mudslide or something, and we swerved and hit a gatepost. He flew off the car and hit the gatepost. He survived, so there was absolutely no reason to change our behaviour.

The other thing I used to do, just for the thrill, was at night I'd drive out onto the country roads around my home and turn the lights off, to see if I could negotiate the roads by memory and not sight. Remember, this is rural Wales – there are no streetlights and it can be its dark-side-of-the moon black. You'd need a torch just to find your own dick. So driving with the lights off is really fucking bonkers. We used to call it 'driving by braille,' because when the car started bumping it meant that you were leaving the road.

Cars were not the only vehicles we used to take us to the edge of death or serious injury. We also used to do all sorts of stupid shit on bicycles. We'd go into the woods with air rifles, on our bikes, and play a fucked-up version of capture the flag, shooting at each other with air rifles while whizzing through the trees. It was like an idiot's version of the speeder bike chase scene in *The Return of the Jedi*. We used to play chicken all the time – my speciality was standing on the saddle of the bike in the street and seeing how long I could stay on before I had to leap to safety. We also used to drive through the local roads on motorbikes. Occasionally the police would spot us and give chase, but we'd simply go off-road and they couldn't follow us. They knew who we were, but we never really got stopped by the police – they didn't really hang out in that part of the world.

In terms of my social life in Cardiff, I had a few friends left over from school so I could hang about with them. I used to socialise with my brother, but to be honest he was a bit of a cock. He was ten years older than me, but I was way more mature – he basically saw life as one enormous, colourful toy. Most of my spare time, however, was spent training.

My training changed a lot once I was back in Cardiff. My real passion then was doing lots of Muay Thai, alongside training in Shotokan karate. The Muay Thai venue was this tiny little gym in B——. I swear the space wasn't much bigger than my living room. But it was a hard-core venue, you know, the metal bucket in the corner of the room for the vomit. We used to do five-minute rounds on the pads, fucking hammering them, the room heavy with the sounds of slapping impacts and grunting effort. Then you'd put the pads down and do five minutes of kicking someone in the stomach, hard. Then you'd swap, with five minutes of someone else kicking you in the stomach or smashing shin again shin. This was proper conditioning – you ended up with a body that had all the resilience of a solid mahogany block. It was fucking brutal and I loved it.

You already know how I feel about karate competitions. I'd batter the opponent, but because he was half a second faster than me, landing punches in my stomach that would've had absolutely no affect in a real fight, he was winning, even though I've managed to smack him in the face. And all I could think was 'This isn't real.' Suddenly I was in this gym with serious fucking characters and they were like, 'You win by beating the living shit out of this person. If he's on the floor bleeding, you win.' That simplified everything.

But this was a good club, with a high standard of training. In fact, it was one of the only Muay Thai gyms that was recognised outside Thailand by the Thai government. It had all sorts of awards and the instructor had lived out in Bangkok, training street kids. He used to come out with some bizarre stories, like the way that some families couldn't afford to feed their kids so they sold them into these Muay Thai camps for training. It was proper knees and elbows stuff, all landed to the accompaniment of that shit piped music – that whiny fucking music like you hear on the TV. I also went from being a reasonably healthy looking lad to being fucking shredded. I could kick better than most of them because of the karate, but what Muay Thai taught you to do was not pull the impact. Instead you'd put your whole body weight into the kick and attempt to cut the person in half or kick their head off into the crowd. For good measure, instead of kicking with your foot you landed the blow with your shin.

I also did a few competitions and I won them all. I didn't do as many as I wanted because I was too busy ripping people off, plus I was doing a lot of high-level karate stuff at the time as well. Another problem was that I liked my beer. I got to the point where I had to decide between doing it properly and professionally or stopping. Unfortunately, tits and beer won. You've got to be really fit to do it. Throwing up was something that happened to you every session. It didn't matter how fit you were, you would vomit by the end of the training.

There was bleed over between my karate and the Muay Thai. As I was running my own karate club at this time, the sessions became a lot more brutal. I ended up delivering this kind of hybrid karate/boxing/Muay Thai martial art – in short, we were shit at *kata* but we would always win the scraps. The Muay Thai experience actually proved quite useful in karate competitions. I was blocking with my legs more. I was also fighting a lot dirtier. For example, I'd drop my weight onto my back leg and then bring my front knee up as the competitor advanced towards me. In Muay Thai, you do a lot what they call 'long knees', and I was using this as a block in karate. So as people came towards me I would raise my legs if I was about to do a front snap kick, but then knee them in the hip. It was a bit of a game-changer technique for me. It slowed everything down – it made people not want to attack you because they got kneed in the hip and it fucking hurt. Some said it ruined my competition technique, but in my mind it just made it more fun.

My mate, John, and me were once in this student championship competition in Chesterfield. Of course, we should have been early to bed the day before, but where's the fun in that? We went out on the piss instead. So the next day, my control might have been a bit off. Nevertheless, I'd got right through to the quarterfinals and I was fighting this student. He was a proper cock, but he'd definitely not been on the lash the previous night. I simply couldn't land a shot on him; he was just too fidgety and fast. I started to get bored of the cunt, so in response I simply ran across the mat, leapt into the air with both my knees up, swinging into him like a fucking wrecking ball. He shit himself and stopped dead on the spot and as I went in I drove my fist into his face. It was like he'd been hit by a running cow. I smacked him so hard that his gumshield went spinning out of his mouth into the crowd – John actually caught it and threw it back, adding some comedy value by hitting him in the eye. It didn't matter though, because he's completely fucking sparked out. Hilarious.

The referee, of course, went fucking nuts and my club instructor didn't speak to me for a week. I think what made it worse for him was that I was still hung over from the night before. But John and I were on a roll, so we actually went off drinking during the competition itself after we met these girls. We were boozing and flirting for so long that we forgot that we were in the finals for the team event. And we were absolutely fucking steaming drunk when we came back into the arena. You have to bear in mind that I was only sixteen at the time.

Evidently alcohol was a bit of a backdrop to my life back then. Our nights out were proper lively affairs. There was one pub in Cardiff near the stadium, and it was dog rough, a right little dive of a place. Me and my mate, James, went in there one night. We were rapidly getting hammered, and I was entertaining myself with two girls on the dance floor, making such a spectacle that the DJ was actually giving a running commentary on what I was doing over the mike. He was making jokes about 'fingers of fudge' – it was horrendous. I was absolutely off my fucking tits. Just to be clear, this was not a classy joint. As I was on the dance floor, I could literally see a guy fucking a girl against the window of the club all while maintaining a conversation with his mate. It was that sort of pub. You couldn't get away with the same sort of stuff nowadays because every place is wired up with CCTV.

Away from the fun, there was some more sinister stuff about my life in Cardiff. My brothers, I have to say, are not the most gentle of folk. One time, there was this guy who owed one of my brothers some money. I had the job of standing guard and keeping watch while my brother smashed this guy in with a lump hammer. Another time, a bloke and his mates pitched up on a building site in a van. They had lots of these boxed-up TVs inside, offering them at such a knock-down price it was obvious they were hot goods. Anyway, we took them off his hands with the intention of selling them on at a profit. We handed over some serious wedges of cash – my brother went and emptied his account and I also handed over two weeks of wages for both TVs and some video recorders.

By the time I got back to *A*— I had sold all the kit. I even sold one to James. I had a big wedge of money, and I was really happy. Then I got a phone call from James's girlfriend saying, 'Conrad, you cunt, you sold us a bust telly! The remote doesn't work.'

So I just said, 'Well get another remote.'

But then James rang me and said, 'You'd better come and see this.' And the TV was literally nothing more than an outer case with a house brick inside to give it some weight. So I ended up giving a lot of refunds and I was apocalyptically pissed off. (Incidentally, I've still got one of those TVs, just for the memories and as a reminder not to be a stupid cunt again.)

In fairness, the man who sold them to us didn't know what he was getting himself into. He just thought that we were thick builders who could be completely outsmarted. What he didn't realise was that he was making a set of enemies who would hunt him down to the ends of the Earth. He could have gone to live with a tribe in the Amazon fucking basin, dressed in fucking grass and bones, and eventually he'd come home from a hard day's foraging to find a fucking builder's van parked in the middle of the camp and me and my brothers piling out for vengeance.

It took us a good three months' deep investigation before we found those fuckers. We looked absolutely everywhere, but they were highly mobile. It turns out that they just spent their time driving around building sites selling dodgy stuff. This actually wasn't unusual at the time. Every week on a building site you would get about three or four visits from vans knocking off all sorts of stuff, such as aftershave and jeans. I remember buying Levi jeans for fifteen quid a pair, when they would have cost at least three times that in the shops. Most of the stuff was coming from ram-raiding. The Welsh Valleys boys would go and smash a car through a shop window, grab as much stuff as they could, and then trail round the building sites the next day flogging it off. But we literally had people posted on building sites all around South Wales looking out for these guys and reporting back. We eventually got their numberplate and a mate of ours in the police ran a check on it and gave us the address. We knew where they lived and they were going to get a visit.

It was bad. We knocked on the door and this guy answered. He completely didn't recognise us – 'What can I do for you?' We challenged him and he denied everything, told us to fuck off and shut the door. Not a good idea. So we knocked on the door again and this time when the guy opened it he had two big lumps of blokes stuck behind him, ready to go. What he had obviously done is make a call as soon as he closed the door and his back-up guys had come in through the rear of the house. My brother, however, was packing quite a tool – he had a half-sledgehammer behind his back. As soon as this guy stepped out of his door, my brother pulled the sledgehammer out from under his coat and smashed it full force onto his collarbone. I heard the bone shatter. Then he got another blow straight across the jaw.

It was the beginning of the most horrendous beating for these three guys – we absolutely mashed them. Then we left, but two days later we went back and gave the head guy another serious hiding, even though he was already all plastered up from his first visit to the hospital.

We spelled out reality for him: 'You fucking listen, we are going to come back every two days and do this to you until you pay us back all the money you owe us.' The third time we turned up, the money was waiting for us, packaged up in an envelope on the doorstep. My brother took the money and we left. But two days later we went back to the house and broke their front windows and smashed the car up. They had to know never to fuck with us again.

In all this, I was starting to realise that I was more handy with my fists than my brothers. Dean was certainly not a fighter, but he was both mouthy and sly. So you would have an argument with him and rather than it becoming a square-on fight, he would simply twat you with a hammer when you weren't looking. So things shifted a little bit and it started to happen that Dean would stay in the van while I went outside and sorted out whoever needed to be sorted.

I wouldn't say I became a criminal in Cardiff, but there was lots of petty criminality going on around me. The levels of thieving got fucking ridiculous. My brother, for example, just can't help himself – if he comes to visit me in my house he'll nick something just because he can. You also have to realise that for some people crime really does pay. The vast majority of criminals are thick as a fat woman's thigh and end up grovelling around on their knees just trying to put some tenners in their back pocket, but there are other criminals I know who are really rich and really smart. These ones, you wouldn't know that they were criminals if you were introduced to them for the first time. There's this one guy I know and he's a proper career criminal. He's got a lovely six-bedroomed house in Essex, he's got an Aston Martin, a couple of BMWs, a Merc, a couple of Ducati bikes, and houses in Spain and Lanzarote.

This is a useful place to interject a bit of education about money laundering, to give you further insight into how the underworld works. There's this Turkish barbershop I know, and if you were to check his accounts you'd think that there were about three thousand people a month going through that shop, all leaving with neatly trimmed hair. In reality, you barely ever see anyone sat in a chair under the scissors. None of the barbers can even cut fucking hair. A lot of the guys who actually work in these barbershops learn just a few basic haircutting techniques off the internet. They learn what the cuts are called, and they like to do the razor cuts because they're actually really easy. In reality the whole barbershop thing is a front for money laundering.

I recently had a run-in with this dodgy business. I took my son down there to get a haircut just before lockdown. He was supposed to be having a short back and sides, but seriously you should've seen the state of his haircut. – he came out looking like his hair had been nibbled off by a goat. It was hilarious for me, but it was devastating for him, because he's a young lad and worries a lot about the way he looks. It looked like a blind man had done it with hedge trimmers. So I went back to the barber and said, 'Look, you've got to put this right.' So he has a go at the hair and then he tries to charge me twice. I start to get a bit vocal. It all starts to get a bit out of hand when he picks up his cut-throat razor and starts waving it about in my face.

I'm not easily intimidated, so I said to him, 'If you don't put that down I'm gonna fucking hammer you.' Anyway, he didn't, so I did. I swear to God that I smacked him on the chin and before he hit the ground there were twelve of his mates around me. His back-up army came from the restaurant was just across the road, run by the same family. All the guys there – big, ugly fellas who look handy – sit outside the restaurant never doing any work. They're all driving BMWs and Mercs. The restaurant is moderately busy, but you never see one of these restaurant guys inside the barbers, until now that is. Luckily, on this occasion I actually knew the guy who owns the businesses, an old fella in his seventies, and he stepped in and probably prevented me from being chopped up inside the barbers.

Barbershops, kebab houses and fruit machines – these are all absolutely brilliant for money laundering. The professional criminal I just mentioned above, he's also got a painting and decorating firm, a building firm, a couple of bars and a burger van. In other words, he's got loads of places to turn dodgy cash into legitimate funds. All you need to do, if you've got illegally gained cash lying around, is just use the legitimate business to take a load of cash transactions. The money is cleaned up and on the books, nicely tabled for the Inland Revenue to look at. Also remember that a games machine, the type you see standing around in every pub, can take about £3,000 in one go, so a criminal can shovel in thousands of pounds of coins and notes every week.

Back to the barbershop example, your barbers might have been sat watching fucking Netflix all day and had about three people through the front door, but on the books it will say that they've been rammed all day. Why do you think that there are so many fucking barbershops everywhere? Next time you're driving down the High Street look into some of the barbershops and see how empty they are, all the time. Some of the chains of barbershops are basically supporting the entire British heroin trade. I heard of someone whose business premises used to be a barbershop, and after he took over he found more than three hundred credit cards stashed in a bag in the wall. Before he moved in there the previous occupants had even found a gun and some ammunition stowed away.

Unless you know what you're looking for, you'd be surprised at what's going on. Late-night take outs, for example, are major hubs for drug dealing and for prostitution. You can order sex in the same way that you can order food, and if the police ask you where this girl came from you can just say that she was delivering food. Prostitution, however, is not as big as it used to be, but the world of drugs is fucking massive. When I was at school I think they were about three kids in the whole school who didn't smoke weed, and I was one of them. I just didn't like it; I don't like the smell. Now every street smells of the stuff. I would also go as far to say that about ninety percent of the people who you see in pubs do coke. It's so easy to get and it can be cheaper than going on the piss for the night, and you don't get a hangover. On one night I saw a group of people who, on the table in front of them in plain view of everyone, had piled up their coke, ecstasy, acid, weed and DMT, and that was just one fucking night. DMT is a new kid on the block and it's pretty fucking horrible. It's a hallucinogenic and it's based on the secretions of those poison dart frogs. The high only lasts for about eight minutes, but it's proper out-of-this-universe stuff, and often really nasty. I've seen people do it and it looks fucking horrendous.

The criminality that surrounded me, however, was a little more benign, if that's the right word. I remember once that my brother got arrested for nicking some ladders. Trouble is, we were doing a roofing job on a big department store at the time and while my brother was getting nicked down below, I'm up on the roof above, unknown to the cops. So, they arrest my brother and take the ladders, then all drive off, leaving me like a right spare dick up on the roof, without a mobile phone. So I was like shouting down to people on the street. I had to get somebody to ring my other brother, who lived way across Cardiff, to come over and bring another ladder to get me down. I was sat on this fucking roof for about four and a half hours, freezing my bollocks off, with no way of getting down. I said to my arrested brother later (after his release), 'Why didn't you tell them I was up there?'

He said, 'Because you are underage, and I'd have got done for that as well.'

'So what were you going to do about me?' (I was getting rattled by this point.) And he tells me that basically he was going to wait until he was released and then come and get me. 'But what if they kept you overnight?'

'Oh, I didn't really think about that.'

Sometimes, in my early years, the police actually targeted me or my family for crimes that we hadn't committed. Like the time they thought we were major bird criminals and launched a full raid on our family home in T—. Some context is needed here. It was back when I was in my teens. We were actually being raided for having illegal pets, but this time there was nothing illegal about it. A mate of my dad was some sort of wildlife rescue expert. I'm not sure how it came about, but this guy had given us lots of fucking owls, which sat in an aviary thing in the back garden. We must have had eight or nine of these hooty fuckers, staring at us with those big uncanny eyes. Indeed, there was a bit of a bird theme going on at our house – my dad used to keep budgies. But then all of a sudden the budgies were gone and basically replaced by owls. (Christ, I hope the budgies weren't fed to the owls.)

I think that one of the binmen spotted the owls and thought that we were robbing eggs, birds, or something like that, and reported us. We had the police rural investigation team come in like they meant business – they literally kicked the front door in. It was really weird, because we knew about the raid seconds before it actually happened thanks to the odd behaviour of my home computer. We had at this time an old Omega computer, which at that time had all the processing power of an abacus, connected to a chunky old-fashioned wooden-framed TV. I was playing a game when all of a sudden I started to get loads of police radio chatter via the computer through the TV speakers, handing out instructions for a raid on our house. We were like, 'What the fuck is that?!' and the next thing is that the front door is smashed in and the cops flood in like they are LAPD SWAT. It was all like *Countryfile* meets fucking *Lethal Weapon*.

Anyway, everything was totally legit (for once) on our side, so they left looking like right twats with my dad threatening to sue them. But then, shit, they found a load of stolen tools on the way out and it all went south pretty rapidly. I didn't really have any dealings with the law until I was about seventeen, and then we saw each other so often we were practically living together.

Although I was training and working a lot in Cardiff, I was also getting into more trouble as well. My lifestyle meant that I was starting to fight more than a special forces soldier in Afghanistan. I was earning somewhere between £300 and £800 every week. So then at the weekends I was coming back to *A*— really wedged up. I had a car, which I shouldn't have had, because I didn't have a driving licence. I also had a mobile phone, which was one of those proper trouser-sagging house bricks of the 1990s. I was spending an absolute fortune on Fila tracksuits, gold chains – I looked like a fucking drug dealer, basically. So when I got out on the town, I attracted trouble like iron filings to a magnet.

When I was back in *A*— all the guys from *T*— used to come out to town, still carrying their vendettas alongside knives and hammers. It got to the point where practically the whole fucking village would try to find me to cause trouble. Every time I was coming into *A*— I was getting into a fight. There were also a couple of times when James had trouble with somebody, but because James had a sensible job, he delegated the violence to me. He'd just point a guy out and let slip that he was causing him problems, knowing that I'd go and sort him out. I'd inevitably go over and find the slimmest excuse to fight the guy.

If someone didn't want to fight me, I had a novel strategy for getting him to overcome his inhibitions. I used to piss on them. Here's an example. There was this bouncer who I really wanted to fight, so I literally just whipped out my cock and pissed on his best Saturday-night trousers – that certainly got him started. Let's face it, if someone pisses on you, you either smack him or you leave. My technique was a guaranteed way either to get them to look like a right dick or to turn it into a full-blown scrap. Either way I won. I used to do stuff like that all the time.

Then I met Chloe.

It began where many of my life events have, in a *dojo*. James and I were teaching a class up at the university. It was the first session of the year, so all the beginners were there, dozens of them in their wavy ranks looking all bright-eyed and excited, forming their own dreams of being a ninja. While James and I were focused on the training, we were also, it has to be said, making a mental note of the pretty girls. And then I saw Chloe. It was like I'd been gut-punched. She was absolutely stunning, really pretty. I casually wandered over to talk to her for a bit, and after a while I went over to my mate, Darren, and said to him, 'I reckon I might end up marrying that one.'

My first efforts to advance this plan hit an immediate roadblock. I asked her out for a drink, but she politely rejected the offer – she had other plans, apparently. But she finally relented when I kept up the pursuit, and I met her in a local bar, me with some of my mates, she with some of hers, for emotional back-up. As I walked in, I spotted her. Fuck, she looked so absolutely stunning, I could barely breathe. The sight of her actually dispirited me a bit. She was just too good for me, completely out of my league. I told one of my mates this and she literally punched me in the face and shouted at me to snap out of it, 'Nobody is too good for you, now get a set of balls and go and talk to her!' Which I did.

The evening seemed to be going okay. In fact, I went back to her flat with all her flat mates and she ended up falling asleep with her head in my lap. It was a good sign. Keeping up the momentum, I went out with her again the following night, and this time all the stars in heaven aligned in the right way for me. I went back to her place and barely moved out again. Actually, the second date was a Thursday night. I stayed with her until Sunday, then went back to Cardiff from Monday to Thursday, during which time I was on the phone to her every night for three or four hours, like a proper love-sick teen. I went back to *A—* on the Thursday night and again stayed until Sunday. I repeated this cycle for about three weeks, then I just couldn't hack even a few days of separation. I gave up my life in Cardiff and moved in permanently with her. We would be together for twenty-five years, bringing three kids into this world. I was just twenty-one years old when we first met.

While my romantic life had just gone stratospheric, regular life had to keep plodding on with its completely dull, fucking lack of imagination. I needed work, of course, and just to add to the list of soul-crushing jobs I've done, I worked for a couple of weeks in a cheese factory. This job was as shit as it sounds, regardless of how much you are into cheese. I didn't like one of the bosses there, and while for some people this might lead to a hard discussion with human resources, for me it inevitably led to us having a scrap during a dinner break. He was a gob-shite and full of his own self-importance.

He was winding me up constantly. I'm not being funny, but it was a fucking *cheese factory* – it wasn't like manning the launch control centre in SpaceX. A trained monkey could've done my job.

I really don't want to sound arrogant, but in places like that I end up either losing my job or being put in charge, because I'm also a bit of a gob-shite and I pick up roles and tasks really quickly. So I ended up leading my particular section, and the guy directly above me just didn't like that. To make matters worse, he was a Special Constable (a part-time police officer), so he knew me from around town anyway and didn't like what he heard.

Anyway, matters soon came to a head. Basically he pissed me off one dinner time – he splashed me with some boiling-hot water. I don't know whether he did it deliberately or accidentally – to be honest, I don't give a fuck. But I did what came naturally. I grabbed one of the metal dining room trays that were used to carry food and backhanded him across the face with it. Christ! The noise that it made when it smacked into his face! As it flexed across his ugly face it generated this hysterical metallic 'dink' sound, like the noise you'd hear in an old *Tom and Jerry* cartoon when Tom gets smashed in the face by something metal. It proper sparked him out. So he's lying flat out on the floor, while I'm collapsing into a fit of giggles at the comedy soundtrack. Of course, when he came to and started to throw about accusations and legal threats, I denied that I had whacked him intentionally. I merely spun around with the tray in my hand and his dull fucking head just happened to be in the way. But everyone knew that I'd hit him. He tried to prosecute me, but all the other lads backed me up so it didn't go anywhere.

So inevitably I lost that job for being a cunt, and things in *A*— were unravelling a bit now. My work was drying up and Chloe also wasn't having a very good time at uni. So we decided it was time to relocate, together, so we headed for a new city. Let's just call it *L*—.

CHAPTER 7 ANGRY YOUNG MAN

Moving to *L—*from *A—* was actually quite a big deal for me. As fucked-up as they were, my family were still my family, and this was really the first time that I had moved away from them properly. We lived for a bit with Chloe's parents, while we were trying to find a flat. That lasted about a week and I ended up wanting to kill them all. Let's just say that they were from a posh neighbourhood and some of them didn't have me in mind when they closed their eyes and imagined a model future son-in-law.

We got this little flat in a place called Monastery Road. Let's just say that it was in a particularly *interesting* neighbourhood. Okay, let's rephrase that, Monastery Road was an absolute shit hole, a half-mile long bin for deviants and dregs. I naively spent everything we had on decorating our substandard flat, but to be honest you can't polish a dog turd. It was depressing.

Also, I couldn't get a job for love nor money. I ended up doing various bits of factory work, agency work, all that stuff. Normally the pattern went like this – the agency got me a job, I went to the job, and then I lost a job. My record speed for losing a job was about four and a half minutes, but on a good day it went up to several hours. At some point during the first shift, I usually ended up thinking, 'Fuck this! I'm going home,' because the work was bollocks.

You want an example? One day me and a bunch of other unfortunates pulled up in a minibus outside a dog food factory. We were meant to be operating meat processing machines. First impressions count, so what do you think our first impression was when we walked into the staffroom area and none of the toilets had doors on them. There were two guys in there both having a synchronised shit, in the open staffroom, talking to each other face-to-face as they crimped one off. It was that type of place. I walked in, saw this, and immediately turned around and walked out. Another time, I was working in a bakery. I thought I'd been in there like a good eight hours, but it was actually only about forty-five minutes. It was so absolutely mind-numbing I could feel my brain turning into sponge, so I fucked off pretty quickly.

I didn't realise it at the time, but in addition to the autism, I've also got the catchily titled attention deficit hyperactivity disorder (ADHD). Sitting around on a production line doing a repeated action all day is nearly impossible for someone like me. If I was bored, it generally led to me doing stupid shit. But eventually I got a job collecting bins for the council, and surprisingly I now found, for the moment, my niche.

Collecting people's waste for a living might should like a real bottom-feeding job to most of you, but I fucking loved it. I got to wander around, talk to all sorts of people, and find some mischief. The wages were absolute shit – I was on £97 a week – and we were walking on average about fifteen miles a day, carrying bins. So it was knackering and poorly paid, but it was also outstandingly hilarious. No two days were the same and it followed the age-old rule – put a gang of lads together and they will get up to all sorts of stupid shit. For example, we once completely filled up a bin bag with black soot and waited for this one guy to pick it up and put it in the crusher. When the crusher compressed the bag, it just exploded all over this guy, like a sooty nuclear bomb. This was like 6.30 in the morning, so for the rest of the day all you could see of this guy was a pair of white, pissed-off eyes standing out in this black face. There was this other guy who I didn't like, and he kept leaving his work boots in the back of the truck. Christ, what a blunder – we filled them with dog shit.

Aside from the silly stuff, our gang also made a fortune through dodgy work on the side. So, for example, we used to go around all the business properties picking up all the commercial waste because it was cheaper for businesses to give it to us than them pay for private contracts. So I was making £97 a week from the council picking up domestic bins, but about £100 a week collecting commercial waste and being paid cash in hand. A lot of other guys would also nick stuff from people's refuse, scrub off all the food waste, and then sell it at car boot sales.

My big problem was money. Chloe was working in retail at this point, and even though we had two jobs, and I was making some cash on the side, we were absolutely fucking skint. Proper poor-people skint, living off packet noodles and ketchup sachets. There was an additional problem. It's called people.

I didn't get on with the people in our immediate neighbourhood. In fact, I tried my level fucking best to stay away from them. We actually lived in one of three flats above a grocery shop. The locals could be described as 'colourful' at best. There was an older couple living downstairs; they were under false names because their children have been taken into care and she was pregnant again. Then there was a young couple in another flat – actually, I say a 'couple' but in reality there were about fifteen of them living in there, illegally. They were dealing drugs. There was actually a murder in the flat connected to the shop immediately below us, while we lived there. Someone broke into the shop and tooled up with one of the heavy weights that you used to put on weighing scales. He then went and caved someone's head in with it. The occupants of the flat immediately next to us were always having parties out in the garden, so people were constantly pissed and fighting. I fell out with one guy from that flat pretty much in the second week after we moved in. Doing my bit to be neighbourly, I ended up headbutting his friend in the face, so they pretty much didn't talk to us after that. Fine by me.

We, on the other hand, were no trouble. We were surrounded by these junkies and smack rats and dodgy bastards, but we had come in and spent lots of money making the flat look nice (or at least as nice as possible).

We were quiet and paid our rent on time. So even to our slum-landlord, we were like a breath of fresh air.

We were there for a few months, and it was rough time. I stuck with the bins for a while, then I 'diversified my portfolio' by going to worked for an agricultural company doing council grass cutting and landscaping contracts. Like the bins, that job was brilliant. I loved every minute of it. It was fantastic because we never really did anything. They would send about eight of us to go and cut a fucking short strip of hedge, a job which one of us could do in about half an hour. At first I got stuck into the task with gusto, but then the boss would slow me down, like calming an over-eager spaniel. The point was, if we did that job quickly the council would expect us to do all the jobs at similar pace. So we would do about twenty minutes work and then fuck off to the chippy, and then another twenty minutes before going down to the pub or heading into the local shopping centre. Or we would go and do private jobs at the same time as being on the council's coin. (You might be spotting a bit of a recurring theme here.)

It was like that all the time. With plenty of spare time on our hands, we got inventive. We would do all the flower planting on roundabouts and things like that. One of our tricks was to spread the bulbs out more widely than we were supposed to and then go and sell the surplus at car boot sales.

The guy I was working with, Alan, was not long out of prison (he'd been involved in some riots and stuff), but he was sound. I think he picked up on the fact that I wasn't happy living in *L*— so he always insisted that I work with him – he was a total mood-booster. The gang in general liked having me around. I was good company, I was handy with tools, and compared to some of the window-lickers that we employed, I was like fucking Einstein. I was with them for three months and in fairness it was great. We used to get double time for any work after five o'clock, which we all did because we were lazy bastards during the regular daytime hours. We would go past all the fresh flower planters in an evening, watering them inaccurately from our moving truck like a toddler learning to piss, just to get the extra cash. Christ, we could stretch it out. We would literally water one lot, go for a pint, water the next lot, go for a pint, and so on. By the time we got home about eight o'clock, we would be drunker than alcoholics trapped in a wine cellar. A lot of our work was around *L*— city centre, so I would also spend a lot of my time down at the shop where Chloe worked, just fucking about.

The next significant phase of life began while I was in this landscaping job. We went out one night in *L*— and there was a bit of aggro. Alan got into a scrap in town. Not knowing my background, he was worried, bless him, that I would get hurt. To be fair, he was a big guy in his forties, whereas I was in my early twenties, and I wasn't eating very much so I was as thin as a straw doll. I had something like a 24-inch waist – I was an absolute beanpole. So when it kicked off that night, Alan was genuinely concerned that I'd be crushed like a dick between two bread boards. But then I went for it like a cornered cage fighter and showed him exactly what I could do. He was like, 'Fucking hell, he *is* Welsh!' – that is exactly what he said. (His dad was actually Welsh, and had been a boxer from Caerphilly, as tough as brass-studded leather.)

After this, the whole atmosphere changed in work. I was now one of the lads. There was a lot of subsequent arse kissing, which I didn't really enjoy. They were also involved with a lot of biker-gang activity, and a few of them were dealing drugs on the side, so I became plugged into all the naughtiness. They weren't stealing off regular people, but I have to say if there was anything in a council office that wasn't padlocked in place, it would end up being lifted and thrown onto the back of our van. I never used to do it because at this time I still actually wanted to go into the police or the army, so I had to keep a clean record. But I turned a blind eye to it, but if someone drops twenty quid into your lunchbox, you don't argue.

Away from work, life in our home neighbourhood was becoming seriously challenging. One night, when I returned home from an evening on the lash with the boys, there was some major aggro downstairs. Some lad was kicking the shit out of a girl. I could hear her screaming in desperation and pain, the soundtrack that comes with deprivation and drugs. If there is one thing I can't fucking stand is blokes beating up women. So I go

145

down and bang on the door, to tell them to pack it in. This guy came out all red-faced and wound up, panting from the effort of smacking someone who couldn't fight back. He told me quite bluntly to back off and mind my own business or he would beat the shit out of me. Two of his mates came out to back him up.

Don't get me wrong, this girl was no angel. She looked about twelve, but was quite a bit older, and was always off her tits on drugs. Her boyfriend decided to beat her up when he found her fucking his best mate, an event that we'd heard several times before – but we didn't tell him that. Chloe and I used to sit tight-lipped through the rows and noisiness downstairs, but this time it had gone on too long. Also, because we had recently had a murder downstairs in one of the other flats, we were a little bit anxious about where things could lead.

So I had a bit of a scuffle with this guy, but in the end couldn't be arsed, so left it at that and went back upstairs. The next thing I know he's outside my flat trying to kick the front door in. Now he'd crossed the fucking line with both of his ugly boots. I fly across the room and rip open the door. This guy is stood there covered in blood. It wasn't his. Some of it was doubtless his girlfriend's and the rest was provided by his former best mate, who'd received a group kicking as punishment for having a wandering dick. Anyway, now this guy's telling me that he's going to stab me. Another group of lads appear like an army of delinquents behind him; it turned out that he was connected with a local drug gang.

He started entering my flat, so I brutally threw him out and went back inside, tooling up for my defence against an entire drug gang. But when low-lives aren't fighting someone else they are fighting each other, and for some reason the gang outside turned on themselves in a ten-man brawl in the corridor, with knives and shit.

Chloe was really panicking by this stage, absolutely terrified. I recognised that this was no place for her to be, so I rang her mum and told her to come and get her daughter out of here. When Chloe's mum and stepdad arrived, I walked Chloe out to the car. One of the shit-kicking guys mouthed off to us as we were passing, so I smacked him with a couple of hard face shots – nothing too grim, just a broken nose. This clearly got their backs up, as when I'm bundling her into the car we hear one of them say, 'Let's break into their flat and fuck it up!' Oh for Christ's sake, give it a rest! I tell Chloe's mum just to take her away, and I turn around and head back up – I'm not going to let them demolish my flat, not after all the fucking magnolia I've flung onto the walls over the previous weeks.

I went back inside my flat and stood at the door like a sentry. They were mouthing off about what they were going to do to me and my home, and I was telling them equally bluntly what would happen to them if they tried it. I backed up my threats with some strong visuals. I had a big fucking Japanese *katana* sword stood near the door at the ready. I picked it and walked outside, looking like I fully intended to perform some ritual beheadings. I left the door of the flat wide open and said to them, 'By all means come inside, but you will come out in fucking pieces.'

And they just left. Don't get me wrong, this wasn't bravado on my part– I would have diced them into Rubic's cube-sized chunks if they have come at me, because they were carrying Stanley knives and all sorts of nasty shit. Plus I don't like scummy people. I know that my language and my manner aren't the best, but there is no need for people to be like that. Chloe and I were minding our own business. If they wanted to kill each other, that's fine by me, just go and do it in some anonymous dirty alleyway, not around my flat. There were plenty of other places where they could've had that fight, and they ended up wanting to rob me because I told them to stop making a ton of noise at three in the morning. Whatever came their way after that was their own fault, simple.

Anyway, I now had more than enough motivation to make a rapid change of address and so we moved house that very morning. We got another place at the opposite end of the street. It might have been the same road, but there was a totally different vibe – far more chilled, respectable and friendly. Problem was, I still hated the way my life was going. My contract with the landscaping company had come to an end, and I just couldn't get another decent job. I did all sorts of menial shit work instead. I don't look down on that sort of work, but I was determined that I was not going to burn up my best years on the ground floor of life. I had been a skilled roofer previously and I knew my way professionally around a building site. I had handled major corporate projects, but here I was washing fucking dishes. Furthermore, I couldn't get a job as a bouncer around here because all the clubs thought I was too soft and too small, which was hilarious as most of the guys on the doors were a joke. They couldn't fight their nan for the last cake on the plate. We were also skint and started to get behind on the rent, so we couldn't go out and we couldn't do anything social to lift the gloom. I was even missing my family.

Looking back, I realise that I was not in a good place, nor was I a nice man to be around. I was bitter. Compounding it all was the fact that I didn't fit in with Chloe's friends either. I had filed them all under the category 'posh cunts'. They all had very nice cars and Daddy had lots of money to bulldozer life's obstacles out the way in front of them. None of them were like me – when we got together it was like *Shameless* meets *Beverly Hills 90210*. All the lads were pretty and sensitive, with fancy hair and three-hundred-quid trainers. Then there was me, with my forty-quid Nike knock-offs and gold earrings, my skinhead, and tattoos. I just didn't go down very well with the crowd.

On nights out, they were like a bunch of little fucking toddlers. I remember one night we were all waiting for a taxi. There were six of us – four boys and two girls – and these two pissed lads came up and started getting a bit mouthy with Jodi, Chloe's friend. Unlike the others, I'm on familiar territory here, so I stood up to the intruders and told them to fuck off. Then one of them put his hand on Chloe, getting a bit familiar and testing my limits. Time to give him one last chance. I explained to him in no uncertain terms that if he didn't fuck off now, I was gonna turn his face into a mixing bowl full of fruit salad. He didn't take the message, so I absolutely walloped him, a clean shot to the face that sent him straight to the floor. I put the boot a few times while he was down, just to make sure that he stayed there while I dealt with the other fella.

Optimistically, I was initially expecting that the other three lads in our group would jump in and back me up. But this just didn't happen. They basically puckered up inside their own arseholes, scared by the nasty people. So I quickly grabbed the other intruder and ran his head into a door post near the taxi rank. Problem solved.

You wouldn't believe the horror on the faces of the people I was out with (or maybe you would). Chloe was simply rolling her eyes, as she knew where all this was going from the first moment these dickheads started getting difficult. Jody was open mouthed – she'd call me something like a 'rabid bull', which in my world is verging on a compliment. And the lads in our group looked like they'd just caught me fingering their mums. So I rounded on them, 'What the fuck is wrong with all you cunts?'

They were like, 'What's *your* problem? You've just assaulted somebody.'

I replied, 'Well he just grabbed my missus and was inappropriate to one of your other friends.'

They said, 'You don't need to settle it with violence.' I'm now thinking, 'Are you fucking serious?' And here lies the difference between me and Chloe's friends. The sheer horror on their faces was astounding. I just looked at Chloe and said, 'Your friends are all faggots,' and walked away.

This was a big incident for us as a couple. Suddenly Chloe's friends didn't want to come out with us anymore. This suited me because they're a bunch of wankers, but it was hard on her. Jody invited us out again – she was a lovely girl – and we went out with her and her two gay best friends. But I just couldn't do it. I'd been brought up in a very different time and community, and I'd never really met anyone gay before. I didn't particularly like them, because in my family being gay was just wrong. I couldn't get my head around it, so effectively we stopped going out with Jodi.

In an attempt to build other bridges, we actually started spending a bit of time with the guys I was working with, but here the problem was in reverse. Chloe, equally, couldn't get her head around those guys, because they were all ex-criminals. In my opinion, they were a lot more honest than the others. Chloe's friends were all well-dressed, had lots of money and talked nicely, but they were also doing a shit ton of drugs. Most of my friends didn't do drugs, even though they were dragged up not brought up, and they looked like shit. But they would do anything for you. And I'm pretty sure that if any guy had swung at me in a taxi rank, all of my guys would've piled in to make sure that I was okay.

Unsurprisingly, all of this started to cause a few issues between us. L—, it appeared, was not working out, so I said to Chloe, 'I want you to come back to Wales with me.' So she did.

Back in A—, I spent a couple of weeks living with my parents. This was not a good idea, and probably would have led to murder if it went on too long. Instead, we managed to rent a really nice flat outside the town. Basically, there was the farmhouse, the attached flat with us in it, and absolutely nothing else but stunning countryside around us. This suited me down to the ground, as it gave us a place to decompress. Financially it was a hell of deal, as it only cost fifty quid a week, which was amazing. We got back to A— on the Friday, where I started phoning around my mates, and by Sunday I had another job, on a building site.

In terms of the martial arts, I began training again at a local university club, but my heart wasn't really in at this time. A lot of the people I knew before I left had graded up, and it seemed to me that many of them had basically become like Chloe's friends, and we know how that worked out. So I focused on training myself and doing a bit with a local boxing club. But the job was going really well, we had a nice house, and we seem to be on the up. And then we had a night out, for fuck's sake.

It was a Halloween night. In the United States, Halloween is more about kids and community. In the UK, it's mainly about women suddenly become the most arousing objects of lust ever, once they are dressed up as a hot witch or curvy black cat. Seriously, my dick felt as unpredictable as a Brazilian space rocket on the launch pad. I went out with a big pack of mates and lots of people from the university karate club to a *Rocky Horror* night. Chloe wasn't with us, but I had promised her that I wouldn't get into a fight, as it was becoming a bit more of a theme again since we had returned to *A—*. Old wounds were re-opened and old scores were being settled. I was turning back into a bit of a wild man, in fairness. I'd been in *L—* too long, and I needed to re-assert my dominance over my home turf.

So we are at the club. I'd had a skinful, but I was being super well-behaved, the angel on one shoulder stronger than the devil on the other, for now. Every time I wanted to beat someone into the ground like a tent peg, I reminded myself of the promise to Chloe, and attempted to decompress. But it's like the world knows what I'm up to, and actively tries to fuck it all up.

I walked into the toilets of the club and there was a guy I knew – a friend from the distant past – who was getting beaten up by two lads in there. I actually knew his sister, and he later acknowledged that he had a vague memory of me. So I gripped one of the attackers and threw him out the way, then did the same to the other one. This last fella slipped on the wet floor and went

153

crashing down, so his pristine on-the-pull clothes were covered in piss from the floor. I thought this was absolutely hilarious, I thought I was going to cough up a lung from laughing. I picked up my old mate off the floor. He was really grateful, thanking me profusely for sparing him from a beating. Trouble was, the two guys who were attacking him had now re-grouped and were coming back. This time they had another three mates in tow – they decided as a pack that it was unacceptable to cover one of them in toilet-floor piss, and needed some vengeance.

They certainly wanted to fight. They were mouthing off at me, the guy I had rescued, and also my mate Alex, who had now joined us for the toilet party. I told him that he should go and get reinforcements. I was still aware of my promise to Chloe, so I'm using my fraying diplomatic skills to try to calm the situation down. It looks like I'm failing, the pressure in my skull rising like a gas canister in an oven. Just as it seemed like the situation was really about to kick off, I decided opt for the deterrent approach, in a last-ditch attempt to prevent me battering them. There was this long chrome fitting on the wall; I think it was a kind of anti-splashback device for the long urinal. I turned around and punched this metal piece as hard as I could. It was an impressive blow, even by my standards. I hit it so hard I actually dented it. It obviously made an impression because the group of five lads took one look at this then decided I was a psycho and legged it. Trouble was, I had broken three bones in my hand. I was that pissed that I didn't really notice. I just crunched the bones back into place and went back to the night out. But the pain started to soak through my senses, which is never a good thing to recognise when you're semi-anaesthetised from alcohol. But the important thing was that I didn't fight.

Eventually Alex drove me over to the hospital, where they diagnosed the broken bones. Luckily I didn't need my hand pinning, but wheels of fortune began to spin again. The injury meant that I lost my job labouring on a building site. Now we couldn't even afford our fifty-quid-a-week flat. Chloe had by this time taken on a job in a nursery. She had actually quit university in *L*— to come back to Wales with me, so she was understandably very pissed off at my consistent ability for fucking things up. Ironically, when I returned home to her after that night, she told me that I should've hit one of them instead, rather than break my hand. This wound me up – so effectively I'm now broke because I didn't hit pummel a bunch of right dickheads. I resolved never to do this again. Next time I'm going to smash down any prick who gets in my way.

It was time to add another grinding job to my lengthening CV. So now I ended up working for one of *the* major fast-food burger chains. (There are only basically two options here, and it was one of them.) I worked there for seven or eight months, which based on my previous history was actually quite a long stint in employment. Believe it or not, I quite enjoyed it and I got made a shift manager after about three weeks. I wasn't very good on the front counter – that involved talking to people, and as I've mentioned I'm not keen on them. But I had really fast hands, so I was super quick at making up the food. There were a lot of young students and kids working there. The owner, Henry, actually owned the restaurant, it was a concession, but more important, he was a second *dan* in Shotokan karate, so we used to get on really well. I was fucking fast in that kitchen, faster than most people who worked there. So we never used to get the massive queues. For this reason alone, Henry loved me, so I kind of used to take the piss a bit. But in return, I would bend over backwards to help him out. For example, if some of the kitchen tiles were broken, I would come back after work and re-tile the kitchen on my own time and money. So he used to be a bit more tolerant of me than other staff.

I have to say, the job didn't do much for me physically or morally. I was doing a ton of hours and constantly eating loads of non-nutritious crap. I was also doing bad shit to people's food, a lot. (Sorry all you fast-food fans, you're going to find the next bit unsettling.) An old enemy came in one time, and I was preparing his food. Of course I'm going to do something his meal. I dipped most of his chips into a really stinking mop bucket, and then fried them off. Nice. I blew my nose into a burger patty once, and then covered it over with mayonnaise. Probably the summit of my contamination efforts came when I wiped my arse with a burger bun.

If a person came in and I really liked them, I'd give them free food. But if someone I disliked walked up to the front counter, I always took over preparing their food in the back. One of my favourite things to do was to serve the target customer with some abused meal, but actually tell them what I'd done to it. I would do this with a wink and smile, so they would never know if I was joking or not. I served it to them, then I'd go out just when they're about to start, or after they had chomped a good portion down, and say, 'I fucking dare you to eat that, go on I dare you.'

They would then get all angry and say, 'What have you done to it?'

And I would just breeze off nonchalantly, 'Nothing…' If they complained and Henry challenged me, I used to act innocent – 'I'd never do that, of course I wouldn't.' I think he pretty much knew that I would, but he gave me the benefit of the doubt.

I also burned some guy's cock once. The context was that Chloe also got a job in the same burger joint, to help us make ends meet. She was front of house one night on the drive-through ordering till and these two pissed-up rugby players came by. She was on Window One and my friend was on Window Two. I don't know what they said, but I do know that Chloe was pretty upset and uncomfortable about it. I was actually up near Window Two, so I had to work out my revenge plot quickly. So in response I made a furiously boiling cup of black coffee – it was like that super-heated water you get rushing out from vents around underwater volcanoes — then 'accidentally' dropped it into this guy's lap in his car. Of course, I apologised for the accident, even as I watched him squealing like a little girl who's seen her puppy run over. His dick had basically been boiled like a hotdog.

There was another similar incident in which two guys in a car had asked Chloe if they could 'eat her pussy'. When she said no, they called her a fucking dyke. Classy fellas. I naturally took a dim view of this. I was blast-furnace mad — you don't talk to women like that. I told the guys bagging up the order that it wasn't ready and that I would take it out myself. So I walked over to the car with the bag of food in one hand, while my other fist was clenched and cocked. When the guys wound down the window, I asked them what they had said. Cockily, one of them smirked out, 'Nothing.' Boom! I gave him a hefty right cross to the face straight through the open window. I then just threw the food all over the interior of the car. They started to get out of the car, revving up to have a go. I looked at them like Satan lining up two new arrivals for torture, and said, 'Oh please, please get out the car.' Seeing the thunder in my face and hearing the menace in my tone, they widely decided against it. This time I did get an official warning, because Henry saw it. I think I would have been sacked normally, but I told him what they had said and he kind of saw my point.

The social life in the business was pretty amazing as well. There were lots of fit girls and impressionable young fellas, most of them several years younger than me. Because of my reputation around town, they looked at me like I was a rockstar with the keys to the shag bus. In these burger places you would get the occasional bit of aggro, usually from pissed-up lads looking for a bit of nosh to soak up ten pints of cheap lager. It was always me who went to sort it out, so that cemented my reputation amongst the other staff as well.

The only downside to this job was that I got really fat, from eating fast food all the time. Chloe was working in the nursery four days a week, then she would do evening shifts in the burger joint. I would do day shifts while she was in nursery, but then I'd also pick up evening shifts as well, so that I could be alongside her. Now part of the staff deal was that you got a free meal every shift, so that meant I was eating two of those each day. I would sometimes be there from half six in the morning until 9 o'clock at night, not leaving the restaurant. I'm constantly chugging down burgers and fries six days a week. I became a right porky bastard.

But all good things come to an end. Chloe was struggling a lot with the situation. She eventually left the nursery work, then she quit the burger joint as well. I quickly realised that while working there was fun, making up burgers and cooking off fries was not a viable long-term life plan. I also wasn't doing my martial arts training very much at this stage, as one of my instructors was going through a bit of a 'special' phase and I was a bit alienated from the club. So when I got offered a job roofing with one of my brothers in Cardiff, I decided it was time to move on. It would offer me better money and more scope for mischief. My brother had a house in B— which was empty, and I said I would move in there and do it up while living in it. Happy days.

I had worked with family before, but this time it was different. Over the past year this particular brother had built up a really huge building company – they were turning over fucking millions – so the opportunities for being a naughty had scaled up as well. I wasn't actually working for him, directly, but rather for a different brother, as a contractor.

From day one it was just fucking nuts, absolute bedlam. We were handling really big national projects, high-profile stuff. At the same time, we were living in the house in B—, but we only stayed there a few weeks because it was really shit. We got a new flat in Cardiff, and we would live there for three or four years, not far from Cardiff Stadium. This was the time when Wembley Stadium was under renovation, so lots of big national matches were held in Cardiff Millennium Stadium instead. Cardiff was a lively place to be during this time. I was working in the centre of Cardiff and Chloe got a job in Debenhams, working as a make-up dolly.

Life was actually fun. Plus, at this particular time I didn't have lots of thugs trying to kill me. I was still surrounded by insane people though. Every morning on the construction site, lots of the guys would drop tabs of E to give them the energy for doing all the steel working. It also gave them the courage to work at ridiculous heights. So we had bunches of young guys, semi-hallucinating and with eye pupils as wide as gun barrels, wobbling about on steel beams several hundred feet above the ground. I dare say that some health and safety policies were being infringed there. We were sort of half working and half playing, which is probably a bit of a theme in many periods of my life. We would work flat out during the morning, then go to the pubs in the centre of Cardiff for lunch. We would attempt to drink the bars dry, then head back to work until about 4.30 p.m. for an ineffective fifteen minutes, before going straight back into the pub by about 4.45 p.m. So, basically, we worked hard(ish), played hard and spent all the money we had.

At this stage in life, I wasn't really thinking of the big picture, just concentrating on what was right in front of my nose. For example, a household bill would crop up and cost a hundred and seventy quid, so I focused on making sure that that money was available. Oh fuck, I need to go out drinking as well, so I'll need another hundred quid on top of that! No problem. Sometimes my horizons were no greater than earning enough money to buy jeans and a jacket to go out on Saturday night, and the things would probably get ripped anyway during a fucking fight. There was no forward planning at all. We were just scrambling through every day as it presented itself.

I did, however, start to dabble about with some underworld figures. One of my mates was managing the pub next to Cardiff Stadium (the pub I mentioned in the previous chapter). There was a bit of drug dealing going on there. I quickly clocked on that a couple of the doormen were dealing outside the pub, but also one of my mates was paying someone to hand out the sweeties inside the pub. For some reason I can't remember, I wasn't allowed to work the door officially in that pub. Instead they repurposed me as a glass collector, but on the understanding that I could step in and sort out some shit if it occurred. I ended up watching over these guys dealing in the pub and made sure that nothing happened to them. It was a slippery slope.

Some nights were livelier than others. One night there was a jungle music themed event in one of the rooms downstairs. The place was absolutely rammed with bulldog-faced men, easy women and drugged-up headcases. In his wisdom, the pub boss only put four door staff on. We had lots of wannabe Yardies and on-the-up gangsters in there, and it got very, very messy very, very quickly. All of a sudden, the whole room just erupted in violence. (We'd actually taken a ton of abuse all evening, with glasses and all sorts of stuff thrown at us.) A colossal scrap breaks out, and quickly the bar resembles the fucking battle of Fallujah, so much so that the door staff end up calling the police to break up the event. Van loads of cops turned up, ready for war. Trouble is, when they arrived, I was helping the bouncers out, hurling people outside and putting them on their arses. As I was unlicensed as a doorman, I think the pub nearly lost its venue licence over that.

In another incident at the pub, this one guy tried to glass me. Evidently, he didn't think through a plan of attack, and went to glass me with one of those reinforced plastic glasses. It dinked off my head, fucking annoying me but not injuring me. This guy really realised that he had fucked up, but fair play, though I beat the fuck out of him he just wouldn't go down. I don't know what he was on, but I literally hit him with fucking everything I had, and he stayed upright like a SlamMan bag. I almost gave up hitting him through boredom. I do have some grudging respect for people who are shit fighters, but at least have a go.

So while life in Cardiff again had started out quite peaceably, it wasn't long before trouble found me waiting and ready. There were also a few altercations on the building site. My brother started not paying people for work, so we had rough contractors turning up on the site all muscled up, trying to find him. Trouble is, at the end of the day he is still my brother, so I stood up for him. Back then, I thought I was supposed to be loyal. We would end up scrapping with all sorts of head cases on-site, slugging it out with fists and tools before taking our bruises and cuts back to work. They were rough days.

I wasn't happy at home, and this situation fuelled the fighting even more. I was pretty much working seven days a week and not getting paid properly because my brother's business was going under (he had been embezzling money and doing all sorts of other dodgy shit). I was working like a bastard from seven in the morning sometimes until about eight at night.

Chloe also wasn't doing too well. She was fighting some demons and general life, not least because I was getting resentful and angry. I would finish work, for example, and would desperately want to go out, but she just wanted to stay indoors, hiding away from the world. She hated B——. She had gone from quite an affluent village with her family down to the arsehole of Wales. We weren't in a particularly great part of the town anyway. Plus, she had to cope with the fact that I was working around the clock, which wasn't great for a couple already starting to talk about the possibility of getting married and having children.

To make matters worse, I also ended up looking after the twelve-year-old kid of one of my brothers. This brother was married, but his wife was an absolute pisshead and he had caught her shagging one of his mates. Their marriage had broken up and he was working away all the time, and as she was incapable of looking after the kid that job fell upon me. Trouble is, he was a bit of a twat and very disrespectful to women, Chloe included. So it was an absolute handful to have him in the house with us.

The pressure was building up inside me, once again. Given everything that was happening, why wouldn't I opt to go out occasionally, get shit-faced with my mates and have a scrap? On top of that, a few of the boys were dealing pills. I actually wasn't into drugs, in fact, I hated them and didn't really want any part of that scene. But if they needed somebody to bodyguard for them, I was always up for some adventure. It was all very unofficial at this stage. I'd just hover menacingly in the background, watching their backs as they did business. This would become something much bigger over time…

I eventually stopped working for my brother (the fact that my wages kept coming in late gave me additional motivation at leave) and went and got a job in a bar instead. It was a rough venue, a typical working man's pub on the docks with lots of hard corners soaked with decades of blood and ale. The doors would open up at half eleven in the morning. As you swung the doors open, there you would find the same eight or nine blokes queuing to get in, eager to calm the shakes from yesterday's pints. They would spend the entire day in there, drinking without break and watching the horse racing. Then you'd get dealers coming in, playing pool and selling their pharmaceuticals.

The staff were as rough as the customers. The supposedly pretty barmaid who worked alongside me, for example, had a face that looked like it had been gravel-rashed. She was the typical nineteen-year-old local girl whose jeans are too small, earrings too big and has a sixty-year-old boyfriend. The landlord had no front teeth from all the fucking speed he put inside himself. He would start drinking at 12:30 p.m. because, God forbid, it was rude to start drinking before noon. Then he would be pissed all day. It was that sort of place. Given the fact that he was mashed for most of the time, I quickly ended up running the entire bar for him.

It was a really busy pub – in fact it was the third highest earner for a major brewery. The weekends were absolutely fucking rammed, a hothouse filled with slappers, gangsters and scroungers.

I was now back training at the Muay Thai gym plus doing karate under some seriously good instructors. For once I was eating right (I think it took me months to shit out the last of the burgers) and training lots, including doing some weights, so I was getting back into shape and good health. I had a lot of testosterone going to waste, and I just piled it all back into my training.

As I got sharper, I ended up doing more of the door work on the pub. I would not be alone. There was a big guy who used to come and drink at the bar. He was really very polite, and he was the only other person in the bar apart from me who could speak any Welsh, so we had that in common. He apparently had a bit of a violent streak about him though. So while nobody in the local area was afraid of me, at least at first, they were absolutely terrified of him. Turns out he was a bare-knuckle boxing champion and he started working the door with me. Fuck he was as a hard as a cast-iron tombstone. He had quick hands and he was strong, but he could also take a beating – some people can naturally absorb a pounding and keep on fighting, and he was one of them.

I fell out with him in the end because he used to hit women though. In fact, there was a woman he was seeing regularly, and every few weeks he would smack her in the face in the pub and I didn't like that. They would go out drinking together, but the problem was that she would pretty much open her legs to anyone else in the bar when he wasn't there. When they were together, she would start flirting with some other guy and he would end up filling him in, then turning on her. As is the way, though, by the next day she would be acting as if the beating hadn't even occurred. Sad stuff.

He also used to do lots of silly shit. One bank holiday weekend the bar was absolutely packed, and he thought that he would liven things up a little bit by walking through the crowds and between the tables spraying lighter fluid everywhere. Then he lit it, and this long line of blue flame just went ripping through the bar, causing absolute chaos. The whole bar stank of lighter gas, spilled pints and singed hair.

He just wasn't quite right in the head. Eventually he wasn't really allowed to go back on the doors because he had done too much stupid shit, so I basically filled his place. I was on my own most of the time and this was a really vulnerable place to be.

I wouldn't exactly call my life rootless, but I have bounced about from place to place a bit. There seems to be a lifespan pattern to each place I live. At first, all is going well, but then violence and darkness steadily creep in and intensify, like living with an abusive partner who doesn't show their true colours for a few months or years. Eventually, the situation would reach tipping point and I would call it quits and move on.

It was happening again, but at least our time in Cardiff was ending on some upbeat notes. Chloe and I decided to get married, and happily we found out that the house that we had been living in for only two-and-a-half years was now worth three times more than what we paid for it. The golden goose had laid a massive fucking gold egg. It was time to bank our chips, so we fucked it all off and went back to *L—*.

CHAPTER 8 FULL POSH, PROPER DODGY

Chloe and I finally got married in December 2002. Chloe's parents oiled the wheels by effectively paying for the whole thing. I think that they were made up that we weren't living in sin anymore. What they couldn't do, bless them, was use money or a wedding to turn me into a model son-in-law.

About a month before the wedding, we were building up to my stag night. Given my legendary abilities for turning even a quiet night out into alcohol-fuelled orgy of chaos, my actual stag night promised to be a proper riot. So we set a decent interval between it and the actual wedding – two weeks. We were going to hold it down in Cardiff. My mate, John, who was to be my best man, turned up a day early, ready to rock 'n' roll. So at ten o'clock in the morning, we decide it was a reasonable hour to go out on the piss, bearing in mind that at this time I was actually still managing the pub down in Cardiff.

By about dinner time, I was taking regular shots from the beer sniper, dropping to the floor with the impact of each fresh pint. All hell was breaking loose and, to compound the problems, I had fallen out with John – he kept trying to shag my barmaids. No amount of lager could stem his appetite for shagging most land-based mammals. I was definitely in the Cunt Book with Chloe, because her parents had turned up early – she wouldn't let me back in the house because I was such a mess.

It was getting late, and I was walking down from the pub to go and get some food. I was, at this moment, alone – I'd become separated from the rest of the stag pack. Alone and pissed – that's when you're most vulnerable. That night would be no exception.

There were some guys I had beaten up a few weeks before, on the door. You always get the 'I'm coming back to get you' bullshit after you've given someone a kicking. Usually, however, it doesn't happen. But this time, the group had decided to follow through. A car suddenly appeared by my side, and this guy climbed out of his car with a couple of his mates, ready for business. He was a right teenage scrote, and came storming over towards me mouthing off, ramping up the energy through the typical pre-attack ritual.

I responded with what I do best. I unleashed a real Saturday-night special right hook straight into his gobby face, which sent him down like a shot dog. I can remember thinking at the time that I was glad I had connected. I was so pissed and I had put so much force into it I would have fallen over if it hadn't made contact with his skull. Honestly, I could barely stand up I was so pissed. So his mates in the car now decided to get stuck in.

Considering I was so hammered, I was actually doing alright against them, holding them off and landing some shots. Another detail I should add is that I was tooled up with a knuckle duster, a nasty spiked fucker that I used to carry with me everywhere in those days. It was a form of insurance against all the people I had pissed off working on the doors. Once I had dominated this group of dickheads, I had enough presence of mind to lean over the lead guy on the floor and tool him up properly with the knuckle duster. It was a good job that I almost semi-conscious, because if I wasn't I would have probably killed the bloke. I was literally straddling him doing a ground-and-pound.

But my brain by this time was in a spotlight, unaware of what else was going on. While I was pummelling this guy into mush, I didn't notice a second car pull up and loads more guys leap out on the attack. One of them just sprinted across the road and delivered a fucking killing blow in my face with a baseball bat, like my head was a ball he was trying to knock out of the stadium. I remember being on my knees smashing the guy on the floor and then looking up at the last minute to see the bat whistling towards my face. I can also remember that I thought, quite calmly, 'Fuck, this is going to hurt.'

Guess what? It really did. It was like I'd had a fucking stroke at the same time as being kicked by a horse. I can remember getting to my feet and there was blood everywhere. I could see the knuckle duster still on my hand, also dripping with blood. Then I notice two people running down the street towards me. I'm thinking, 'Now I'm in trouble', so I sprint off down a side street. I was also starting to realise that my face was in an interesting condition – I could actually see my lips out of my peripheral vision without looking down and pouting. The impact had basically split my face in half. I legged it down the side street, the survival instinct giving me an adrenaline shot. When the people chasing me got level, I stepped out and smacked them really hard in an ambush, only afterwards realising that it was John and another mate. Luckily I didn't hit them with the knuckle duster; I gave them hard lefts instead.

Once all the proper identifications were made, and some pissed-up apologies, they got me to hospital. I was so out of it from the alcohol and the injuries that I couldn't really explain what had happened to me. I also arrived at the hospital with my hands hidden inside my jacket, because initially I didn't want people to see that I had a tooth sticking out of one of my knuckles. It was rammed hard in there, and was preventing me taking off the knuckle duster. Luckily the doctor in the hospital was a really good guy who'd seen it. He removed the tooth and passed the knuckle duster to John, telling him to get rid of it because the police were on their way.

My face was like the aftermath of an earthquake. I sat in accident and emergency trying to eat pizza – it would take more than major facial injuries to put me off my food – sucking the cheese in through a hole in my lip. Believe me, my lips knew it when they found the only chilli in the pizza. I leapt off the hospital chair then collapsed on the floor. So they rushed me through to assessment and surgery.

The doctors called for a reconstructive surgeon that night because my lips no longer aligned. Even today, if I don't have a beard or moustache you can see that my top and bottom lips don't really square up properly. So the surgeon had a go at sorting it all out and stitching me inside and out. My four front teeth had been knocked out, spoiling my super-model good looks. This really pissed me off because I just spent serious money – about £4,500 – having them reconstructed from losing them in an earlier fight. I also had a fractured cheek bone.

I spent the night in hospital getting stitched up and patched up. When Chloe saw what a state I was in, the marriage was basically called off. Her parents were pretty happy about that – I didn't exactly look like the society husband lying in hospital stinking of booze with my face smashed in.

Against the odds, however, the wedding did go ahead, but it was a predictably messy day. My wounds had healed just enough for me not to scare kids in the wedding photos, And I looked reasonably presentable. My best man, however, was an absolute dick. I picked John up again from the airport two days before the wedding (he was living in Germany at the time) and he staggered off the aircraft absolutely pissed. I didn't see him sober at any point for the next two days. He woke up at two in the morning on his first day in the UK, and went into the kitchen in my house and drank two bottles of champagne straight down, because he was thirsty. He was that pissed. On the wedding day itself, he basically didn't do his best-man speech because he was too pissed to form words properly. He then disappeared for half of the evening reception because he was shagging my wife's cousin behind the village hall. To be fair, she was a fucking mess and her standards had dropped well low by the time of the wedding. The whole thing was grim. But, by the end of the day I was married to the woman I loved, so that was sorted.

After we had sold the house in B—, Chloe and I actually decided that we were going to travel for a bit, to let off some steam abroad. We had our eyes set on the United States. We went off on our honeymoon in January, got back from that and put our house on the market. Within a week of doing that it had sold, and my arse was now happily sat on top of a big pot of cash. We packed up all our shit and drove to L—. Our plan was to put all our stuff in storage and head off to the United States. But as so often, life erected a massive fucking STOP sign, complete with flashing lights and speed cameras. Chloe's beloved great-auntie got really sick with cancer, so we decided to stay and help out with her care while she went through her last weeks. We both got part-time jobs to tide us over. The great-auntie died a couple of months later, but by that time Chloe was pregnant with our first child. So we decided to stay put.

We had already lived in L— once and I swore that I would never do it again. The difference this time was that we had a fuckload of money in our account. All of a sudden it looked like a very different city. We didn't exactly handle our new-found wealth maturely. We did a lot of partying and bought a ton of expensive toys. But evidently God thought that it was time to invest in my spiritual life, as I got a job at L—'s magnificent cathedral.

I was working with the masonry department as a sawyer mason. A sawyer's job is basically to extract a piece of rock from the ground and prepare it and approve it for use by a stonemason. We were basically pulling raw rock out of the ground, squaring it off and carrying it about on a forklift for use in masonry work in the cathedral. It wasn't really like a real job. In my previous employment in building, you were always working to punishing deadlines (even if we constantly fucked about with them). At the cathedral, the only timetabling principle was, 'do it when you can' – apparently God's work is really leisurely. I found that I spent a lot of my days doing martial arts training or reading magazines.

Most of the actual working was spent down the quarry. This was still laid-back stuff. You could spend an entire day preparing a chunk of stone, just to find a minor flaw in it and have to bin the entire piece and start again. If you had nothing to show for your time at the end of the day, that was perfectly acceptable.

You might think that working in a cathedral limited the opportunities for dicking about. Apparently not. They didn't really have to give me any training because I already had my forklift licence when I got there. And then they realised that I was qualified in safety netting and other procedures, which nobody else was. At that time, they were doing lots of high-up work on the cathedral, so I was able to put all the proper safety procedures in place. And that, my friends, meant that I was effectively a law unto myself. So when I was bored I spent quite a lot of time fucking about in the quarry doing stunts with the forklift truck. We used to make courses and then race the forklift around it, doing goofy time trials between us. I didn't really do a lot of work if I'm honest, especially as the wages were predictably shit, but I didn't care because I still had money from the sale of the house.

Some of the more secular staff in the cathedral used to call me 'Fuck Off'. Every member of staff at the cathedral had to wear a lanyard with an ID card, but I never used to put mine on because it would dangle – that was a danger around safety netting. So every time I walked into the cathedral they would try to charge me, and I would just tell them to fuck off. I said it so many times that it turned into a name that stuck.

There were a few random hilarious moments during this whole time, like when I went around to the bishop's house for tea. It was the bishop's annual BBQ one weekend, and the masonry gang had been invited. The barbecue was scheduled to kick off at four in the afternoon, so naturally we all went to the pub at 10 a.m. By the time we turned up at the BBQ, we were stumbling and only semi-coherent. Quite frankly, if you want me to behave at any event, don't let me have access to drink for at least six hours before it.

At this particular event, amidst the gentle conversation and cakes on doilies, I actually ended up headbutting one of the other stone masons in the bishop's back garden. He threw the first punch though (the stone mason, not the bishop), so it was fine – he was under the impression that I was a bit soft, and fancied his chances. Basically he was being a bit of a dick and I was being a bit of a dick, and we met in the middle of all the dickishness. He threatened me and I initially backed down, keeping up appearances. But I then he followed him to the bottom of the garden and when I thought nobody was about, I nipped over to him and headbutted him in the face. I didn't realise that everybody in the place had actually seen what happened. I'm strolling back up the garden, pretending to be sober and responsible, when they've just seen me flatten this guy's nose. We actually turned out to be friends in the long run.

I worked at the cathedral for about three or four years, and while I was there my life took a major new direction. I began teaching karate again, seriously. I was contacted by a leading KUGB representative. I had actually been looking around for a class to join and I was told by the KUGB that the nearest one was at G—, but the instructor had fucked off. So I was asked to take it over, but it was actually about an hour's drive each way so I couldn't be arsed. At the same time, I was doing a lot of weights and fitness training at the local posh gym, you know, the type of place that's as much for posing as for getting fit. One day, a gym instructor wandered over, interested to find out what I was doing – I was using the speed ladder to do kicking drills. He saw that I was very quick on my feet for a big lad. A few of the other gym instructors also began to take an interest. Inevitably someone in the gym recognised me from my regional karate squad training. It ended up that the manager of the gym asked me if I would run an eight-week karate course there. And they paid me a fuckload of money for doing it. Eight weeks, two hours a week, and I got paid the equivalent of four months of wages at the cathedral. I was in there anyway and I got a free gym membership to boot.

It turned into a long-term thing. The eight weeks passed and all my students graded successfully. I actually ended up with about forty students in my class by the end of the period. But this was just the beginning, as it turned out. I was soon doing a kid's class and an adult class back-to-back on a Sunday morning. This really suited me because, Chloe, who was pregnant at the time, would also come in and use the pool and other facilities, then we'd have lunch in the fancy club restaurant overlooking the tennis courts. We had slipped into a very upper-middle-class lifestyle, moving from South Wales from what was basically the fucking ghetto to a nice house in L— and mixing with the upper echelons of society. We were soon also driving around in a gorgeous little MG Midget convertible.

As I was on a roll, I also started teaching karate around the cathedral. L— itself is very focused on the cathedral and anyone with money makes a point of worshipping there, so I was getting a bit of a good name for myself. Plus, by doing more and more karate, I was managing to stay out of trouble.

Then one day someone came in and asked me to do a martial arts class at the private school connected to the cathedral. This establishment was light years from the schools I had attended. It was super exclusive and smelled of fine leather, waxed oak and books. The kids were basically destined for greatness just by being there. The school asked me how much I would charge to teach, per person per term. I replied that I didn't really know because I hadn't thought about it, plus I wasn't sure if I could get the time off work. So I went and spoke with the cathedral authorities. They asked how many afternoons I needed to take off to do this. I said about two a week. So before I knew it, I was teaching in the school. It was just one of those beautiful times when all the doors swing open on oiled hinges.

Again, they paid me an absolute, ridiculous, fortune. I was charging per head and I was expected to have about forty members in the class, but a hundred and twenty people signed up in the first term. I ended up quitting my job at the cathedral to teach full time. Chloe also helped me to expand my growing martial arts empire. Because I was only, basically, just learning to read and write, at this time, she contacted lots of other local schools offering my classes for a couple of hours a week, pointing out that I was already the instructor at the exclusive gym and at the cathedral school. Whatever she wrote certainly worked, because suddenly all the local schools wanted me to teach there.

My working day now began at about 2 p.m. I would teach in schools until 5 p.m. Then I opened a class in the village where I was living, and that ran from 6 p.m. 'til 8 p.m. three nights a week. It was like I had become the martial arts equivalent of King Midas, turning everything I touched into karate gold.

There was a kind of cyclical marketing at work here, as lots of the parents of the kids who went to my training classes at the cathedral school heard about my teaching, so they came along to my village classes in the evening. The next thing you know I'm doing four classes a night for five evenings a week and then all day on Sundays. I went from teaching about forty students at the gym for a favour, right up to the point where I think we had about five hundred and ninety students in total, distributed across all the training venues.

I got to the stage where an examiner was coming to me every month to do gradings, although I eventually fell out with the him and took all of my clubs out of the KUGB. I moved my students' memberships over to another organisation, but I really came to regret this. To orientate myself to the new organisation, I took a group of my students to train at one of the leading examiner's clubs. I couldn't train myself at the time because I had broken my hand, so I sent my students in without me. They came out a couple of hours later and told me that the instructor was full of shit. This guy told him that he had known me since I was little kid, which was totally untrue, and they knew it. He was that kind of character – bit of an imaginative twat. But I was making a lot of money, so I let my judgement be affected by that. I was making a fortune, and people noticed. One of the world's most senior karate figures, a revered *sensei* from Japan, actually came over twice to the UK to check out what was happening in my club, and do some gradings – at one point he did fifteen black-belt gradings in one of our sessions.

I was super busy doing this training for about four or five years. I also started to do what we called 'Speed–Power Classes', which were basically Muay Thai-oriented. There were several occasions when me and that senior karate examiner clashed though. I nearly took his head off once in a competition, when he got in the way of a fight just as I had fired off my fist. He used to tell lots of lies. If he was gaining something from this you could maybe understand it, but he used to say shit that was virtually guaranteed to include untruths that people would immediately spot.

The problems began mounting with this guy. Eventually he assaulted one of my students in class, to the extent that the police were involved. There was this girl in our club who was really talented at karate. During a visiting training session with this chief instructor, he told her to try to hit him. Now my students knew that if I said, 'Try to hit me,' then I expected them to attempt to bury me into the wall behind. Anything less, and I would bollock them. So this girl took the same approach with the examiner, plus she was lightning fast. She absolutely walloped him, cutting right through his guard. He repeated this three times, and each time she came in so violently that he couldn't block her.

Now he's starting to get really pissed off, plus he looks like a bit of an incompetent twat in front of the club. What he was implicitly saying was, 'Come in fast and sharp, but actually don't.' But that's not how I train my students. On the third time that he fucked it up, he suddenly lost it and grabbed her and smacked her in the mouth. He split her lips and nearly took her front teeth out. We are talking a really pretty nineteen-year-old girl here. Apparently he also whispered, 'I will fucking kill you!' I didn't actually hear or see all of this because I was at the opposite end of the room training with his second-in-command, but I had to stop the session and kick him out. Her parents called the police, quite rightly so, and I parted company with the organisation that very day. How can you have someone like that in your top ranks? He didn't just do it in front of the class, but in front of most of the parents as well. We are talking teachers, solicitors, doctors – lots of professional parents who won't tolerate shitty behaviour.

So my response was to try to set up my own martial arts organisation with a couple of mates, but it was dog shit. By this time, my heart wasn't in it anyway. Backing up a bit, about eight months before this I had done a corporate team-building day. An executive had approached me in the gym and asked me if I could come into his company for the day and train professionals to do something like break a board. I said no to the board-breaking, which was a good way to fracture soft office hands, but I could do other stuff with them instead. So I spent a full day with these executive types getting them to punch, kick, hit pads and scream a lot. I started to do a few of these here and there, and some breakaway courses.

At the end of one of these courses, a guy came up to me and said, 'I get the feeling that you are a bit handy.' I asked him what he meant. 'Well, there are some people who do karate for fun, and then there are people like you.' I was cagey, because I had been trying to hide all that side of my personality.

'I don't know what you mean,' I replied, but I realised that he must have spotted my inner thug.

'Have you ever thought about doing a bit of security work?' he asked me.

'Well, no,' I responded. He pursued it.

'I know people who need minders.'

Another door was opening, but when it came to actual clients, what he really meant were dodgy car-salesman types. As it turned out, I had actually done a close protection (CP) course some years previously, so I decided to give it a go – I was going to become a bodyguard.

This is how I found myself being paid six or seven hundred quid a week to escort fat dickheads about. One of them was *literally* a dodgy car salesman, a properly unlikable man who needed protection from all the customers who were driving around in his malfunctioning vehicles. Chloe and I used to joke about it, because these clients were suspicious as fuck, but in my eyes they were actually quite harmless. They were essentially the type of people who ran their mouths off and got themselves into a load of trouble. Half the time I was just driving them around. Really, I was there to act like a piece of jewellery, showing how big and important the client was. A lot of these guys just liked to tell people that they had a bodyguard. By this time, my hair had thinned to such an extent that I was effectively a skinhead. My shiny scalp, grizzled facial hair, and selection of tattoos, did give me a visually menacing presence and the clients knew this. I was also about sixteen stone in weight, but most of this was lean muscle. In short, I looked the part.

So now I was doing this security work in addition to my martial arts teaching. The situation began to evolve, however, spreading its fingers into other pies. Inevitably, a guy asked me if I would help him out with an off-the-books problem, specifically extracting money from someone who was refusing to pay him. Basically, he was owed £8,000 from a business partner. There was nothing written down, so he couldn't take him to court or pursue legal action. I said to him, 'Look, I'll get you your eight grand, but you have to give me two of it.' He began to argue, saying my twenty-five per cent rate was ridiculous. I pushed back, reminding him that at the moment he had fuck-all. So eventually we shook hands on it.

I felt that this was a good deal for him, plus I needed the money. All the money from the sale of the house had now been pissed away on baubles and by this time I also had two kids to support. Our mortgage was also a ridiculous high price because I had no credit rating. Two grand to me was good money and he reluctantly agreed to it.

So, I found the guy who owed the money. I marched straight up to him and told him that he owned his former business partner eight grand. He denied it of course – they always do. I knew he was lying, because he kind of smirked and said that we couldn't prove anything. 'Okay, I said, then I left. By the superior look on his face, he thought that he'd got away with it.

I returned later that night with a hammer and remodelled his car on the drive. I totally destroyed it, even though I was only there for about fifteen seconds at the most. I ran over the body work like a fucking machine gun, hammering the panels and anything that was glass. So no one could identify me, I had a scarf around my face and my hood up, proper street ninja. I then fucking legged it like Usain Bolt, totally shitting my pants.

This was just Part 1 of the game. I went back the next day, knocked on his door and asked him again about the eight grand. He looked at me with absolute disbelief. I turned around and scanned the car on his drive and asked him, 'Fuck me, what happened there?'

He immediately fired back, 'You know what happened!'

I put on my innocent, take-your-nan-to-church face and told him, 'No, I don't know how that happened, but the fact is if you fuck around with people, things are going to keep happening to you.'

He went white. 'What do you mean?'

I fixed him with a stare, 'Well, you're lucky they didn't set fire to your house, mate.'

'Is that a threat?'

'No, it's just an observation.'

He was screaming at me when I went down the driveway, and I thought, 'I've fucked this, I'm going to get done.' So I got my alibi sorted and left it a couple of days. In the meantime, he had actually reached out to the guy who had hired me, asking him what was going on. But this got me thinking, 'He hasn't gone to the police.' That's when I knew he would pay up. So I went round to the house again and knocked on the door. When he answered, I told him that this was the last time that I would come around and ask nicely. I was so menacing a fucking ghost would shit itself. After that, anything that happened was his responsibility. Again, he asked me if I was threatening him, but I said no, it was just more of a prediction. 'Your car is fucked, but next time it might be your legs, so you really ought to hand this money over.'

He arranged for me to come back the next day and pick up the money. When I returned, I sat there in the car before I went over to the house, thinking that as soon as I stepped out the car, loads of hidden cops would suddenly rush out and pounce on me. I'd spend the next ten years staring at nothing in a concrete cell. Instead, when I finally walked over and he gave me the money in a little plastic bag, the notes still in the banking slips. Job done.

Over time, I've got very good at knowing when someone will go to the cops or will simply fold and pay me the money. This guy had ripped someone off for £8,000 and absolutely nothing was on paper. That alone told me that he liked keep things away from the law. The guy he had ripped off was also dodgy as fuck – he used to sell cut-and-shut cars. At one point, my target was in partnership with this fucker, which tells me that he didn't strictly operate within the law. My dad was very much the same kind of person, so I had some training in spotting the characteristics. A lot of these people simply don't want the police coming around to their businesses and homes and asking them probing questions about why all this is happening to them in the first place, because before they know it, the tax office and fraud squad will be doing a full investigation of their affairs. With most of the debt collections that I went on to do (many of which we'll explore in volume 2), almost all of it was a case of ill-gotten gains.

This was the beginning of something new. I had my martial arts classes, my bodyguard work and now I had a potentially lucrative new side-line in debt collection. In my first week of doing this, I earned £5,000. And life was fun again – somebody actually paid me to go and play at being full gangster. I found it fucking hilarious. The furtive bloke who had given me my first job had a load of other people who owned him money, so my new-found debt-collection skills were suddenly in high demand. And then he was telling his mates about me.

At the same time as I was dealing with the dregs of society, therefore, I was also rubbing shoulders with some of its most wealthy members through my work at the cathedral. So one minute I'm sat having dinner with top executives and RAF fighter pilots and the next minute I'm in some shitty part of town rough handling money out of proper scum because they haven't paid their drug debts. It was mental. I was going into the cathedral school and basically getting blank cheques handed to me from parents. Sometimes the cheques were from Coutts Bank, the private bank that only accepts high-net-worth individuals. You've got to have about three million, at least, to open an account with them. I'm rubbing shoulders with the bishop of L— and the head of the county police (his kids were my students), at the same time as I'm collecting big wads of dirty notes from some of England's most undesirable citizens.

It was a really weird situation. One time, there was this invitation-only ball connected to the cathedral. Everybody wanted to go to this ball, including Chloe's aspirational parents, but only a select number were invited. Fuck me, I was one of them! I'm on the top table of this black-tie event with the elite of the city, talking with some guy about how he has just bought a dock in the South of France because his yacht was so big he needed to buy the whole fucking dock. Chloe was really well-spoken so often I would let her go off and talk with the toffs while I would slink off into a corner and get pissed. The following day I found myself running around a council estate with a baseball bat. But as monster weird as my life had become, even I couldn't have suspected where it would turn next or have imagined the event that would do it.

CHAPTER 9 TURNING POINT

Ironically, people with lots of money are actually quite similar to me. We share one quality – we detest the middle class. So I generally got on well with the higher strata of society, and they recognised in me someone who could be useful to them. Word had got out that I was handy with my fists, so soon enough I wasn't only looking after low-budget businessmen in shiny suits, but had graduated up to minor celebrities, media industry types and high-achievers who wanted a bodyguard as a bit of a high-fashion accessory.

One of my first clients from this new group was a low-level film producer. Actually, he wasn't much better than the shit-kickers I'd worked for previously. His creative output was absolute crap, you know, straight-to-DVD, dog-shit stuff. I'd got the job basically by being a bruiser in the right place at the right time.

One day, we were at this film-industry party. It was one of those events where you had to display country manners, so neither of us fitted in. To be honest, I think he had paid money to squirm his way onto the guest list, rather than be invited. Anyway, he decided that to get through the evening and work the room more efficiently, he needed to buy a metric ton of coke and snort it up his nose. He hit me up for a few of my contacts in the underworld. I felt it was a bit scummy, but what the fuck, I gave him the numbers.

We got him sorted, but then later in the evening, when we were outside in an alleyway, two guys tried to rob him for the drugs. I give them this, they were initially ballsy fuckers, as they attempted to mug him even though I was there. One of the guys came round the back of me and hooked his arm around my throat. The other guy did the same to my client, although he ramped up the threat with a knife in his hand. Now I didn't know it at the time, but the guy who had grabbed me also had a blade – a Stanley knife was hovering millimetres above my windpipe, I just couldn't see it. To be frank, my threat-awareness radar might have been reduced by the multiple pints I had knocked down through sheer boredom at the party. I know this doesn't sound very professional, but to be fair my client was an absolute fucking clown so there wasn't much respect.

Once under threat, however, I reacted fast. I whipped my heavy skull straight back into his fucking face, wrenched his arm away from my throat and then hip-threw him hard to the floor. As he slammed into the concrete, I spotted he had the knife. As soon as I saw this, I've got to admit, I might have gone a little bit psycho on him – stamping on his face, stamping on his hands to break his fingers, smashing up his legs. I literally football kicked every fucking part of his body that I could find. He was out for the count and his villain mate was frozen to the spot in terror. They thought that just because they had a couple of knives I would shit myself and roll over. Instead, when I had finished (temporarily) with his mate I simply walked over to the other guy, grabbed his knife and then caved in his face with a head butt.

This was proper bodyguard shit. Two guys had tried to rob my client, but now my only concern was that at least one of them might fucking die, or at least face a future involving wheelchairs and round-the-clock care. Every time I went to walk away, I would suddenly rethink and go back and batter the first guy some more, because I was so pissed off.

Anyway, the upshot of this scrap was that several influential people had seen me in action and word got about. About three or four days later I got a phone call. I was asked to bodyguard for a well-known, hot, Hollywood actress, a proper big-screen film star, who had a stalker. (Sorry guys, I really can't name her.) Fuck me, some people network their way to success. I did it by battering people.

This job would prove to be a total game-changer.

They initially wanted me to go and meet her, but I couldn't because I was working away at the time and I wasn't impressed enough by celebrity just to drop everything. But she was obviously keen to have me protecting her because a couple of days later she turned up on my home doorstep. I've got to say, she looked out-the-ballpark stunning. She was wearing a baseball cap, a sweater and a pair of jeans that look like they had been spray painted on. To be honest, I've met a lot of Hollywood celebrities who look fantastic on screen, but when you meet them in person you actually think, 'Is that it?' Well this girl was not one of them. Even in person she was a level fucking eleven.

She was also extremely flirty. We were out in town together as part of the process of getting to know each other, and she commented on how awkward I was looking, so she hooked her arm into mine. I told her that I was worried that she would be recognised. She responded, 'I'm walking about L— with you, who the hell is going to recognise me in this context?' One person who did recognise her, however, was my sister-in-law, who photographed us from the back and then sent the picture to my wife, although I explained that I wasn't doing anything dodgy. At one point in the evening, when we had both had quite a lot to drink, she was stood outside a Wetherspoons dancing with two fucking homeless people. That was the most surreal moment, especially as the homeless guys didn't actually realise who they were dancing with.

She was quite willing to use me as a useful prop to get out of awkward situations. One time we were drinking together in a bar and some guy persistently tried to chat her up. To wiggle out of it, she wrapped her arms around my neck and said, 'I'm taken.'

Most of my duties with her involved going out for drinks or taking her out shopping. I was super protective of her, as she was obviously vulnerable – as you'll discover in the next book, most celebrities are really unhappy people. I didn't like others talking to her, and I certainly didn't like guys hitting on her. Sometimes she would ring me at two in the morning just for a chat, or she would end up talking to my wife for hours to calm some of those late-night fears.

I quickly realised that the people who hired me didn't really want a conventional bodyguard. Rather, they wanted someone a little bit dodgy would essentially go round and batter this stalker fella. He was an ex-boyfriend within the industry and he was a proper cunt. I'm not going to name him, but let's just say he now has only one eye. You'll see why, shortly. I'd do things like accompany her to film sets or take her to important industry parties where he might be there.

There was some discussion about how we were going to sort this guy out. Well-bred media folk discussed all sorts of complex strategies, but I suggested simply going around to his house and battering him, which I did. But weirdly that didn't stop him. In fact, his next fucking delusional step was to try to intimidate me, a move that was not going to work out well for him. He thought that his success in the industry would be intimidating, and in various ways he threatened to ruin me. He obviously didn't realise that I don't give a shit. I'd got to where I was by the skin of my teeth and I didn't really care if I stayed there – I'll keep swimming in whatever sea I find myself. He was, however, making me really fucking mad. To be perfectly honest I couldn't stand the man, so I probably would have hit him for free.

Matters came to a head at an awards party. It was the usual event, packed with well-to-do industry types all chinking their crystal glasses and playing to the gallery. The stalker guy was there, and when he started to get a bit forward, I decided it was time to throw him out. I dragged him out from the room, bouncing him off a few tables on the way. In front of all his peers, I humiliated the shit out of him, and threw him out onto the street like I was fly tipping him into a ditch. But he just didn't know when to quit. He slipped the door security a few quid to let him back in again. This time he had the red mist in his brain. In his delusional fucking world, he decided that he was going to sort me out, physically, in front of all the guests and re-establish his position in the hierarchy.

Suddenly I notice him sprinting across the room towards me, looking fucking insane. I had wound him up so much that he had picked up an empty glass – he was intent on glassing me. The few seconds it took for him to cross the room which allowed me to set up the perfect shot. As soon as he came into range, I just side-stepped and hit him with a single punch that had the same power as a fucking elephant gun. It was fast, it had my whole bodyweight behind it, plus he added his own forward momentum to the impact.

I don't think I've ever unleashed such a devastating punch. It really hurt my hand, but it actually caved in the whole right side of his face, including his eye socket. It was bad, really bad. He was actually on the floor twitching and shit, so I'm wondering, again, if I've killed somebody. This didn't stop me from putting in the boot a couple of times just to make sure he wasn't getting up. I know what would happen if you put me down on the floor and let me get up again.

So, the problem of the stalker was solved for good. (He survived, by the way, but really got the message.) Because he had charged at me with the glass, I was able to escape any legal repercussions through justifiable self-defence, which, given the damage a person can do with a glass in less than a second, it actually was.

This incident was a transitional event for me in many ways, both good and bad. On one side, it would open up many more doors to me in the film industry, where I would eventually work in all sorts of roles, including stuntman, fight coordinator, weapons trainer and even, on occasions, actor. On the other side though, it also led me a little bit more down the criminal path. High-powered people had now seen how I could solve problems for them, and suddenly my phone began to ring a bit more. If you want to find out what those people wanted me to do, you're just going to have to buy the next volume.

As I said at the very beginning of this book, it's only now that I realised that my journey from childhood to adulthood was not normal by nearly anybody's standards. But the fact is, I'd survived. I'd picked up some solid fighting skills, a combination of endless hours of martial arts training plus the steep learning curve of actual street violence. My body had taken and given thousands of blows, but it was still standing. I had built successful businesses from scratch, and acquired celebrity clients. For someone who left school barely able to write his own name, I'd done alright.

It wasn't all roses, though. The traumas I'd experienced along the way were not all gone. They would remain locked in a tight, black, metal box in the basement. I thought that I'd thrown away the key to the box long ago, hurling it with all my strength into the grey and choppy sea I'd spent so much of my life living next to. But it would wash back up on the shore later in life, although I have never backed down from facing any enemies, mental or physical.

For now, however, the world was starting to give me some serious respect. Even I couldn't imagine where it would take me next.

Printed in Great Britain
by Amazon